▶ **The Dynamics of a Terrorist Targeting Process**

Palgrave Hate Studies

This series builds on recent developments in the broad and interdisciplinary field of hate studies. *Palgrave Hate Studies* aims to bring together in one series the very best scholars who are conducting hate studies research around the world. Reflecting the range and depth of research and scholarship in this burgeoning area, the series welcomes contributions from established hate studies researchers who have helped to shape the field, as well as new scholars who are building on this tradition and breaking new ground within and outside the existing canon of hate studies research.

Series editors:

Neil Chakraborti
University of Leicester, UK

Barbara Perry
University of Ontario Institute of Technology, Canada

Series advisory board:

Tore Bjørgo (Norwegian Institute of International Affairs); **Jon Garland** (University of Surrey, UK); **Nathan Hall** (University of Portsmouth, UK); **Gail Mason** (University of Sydney, Australia); **Jack McDevitt** (Northeastern University, USA); **Scott Poynting** (The University of Auckland, New Zealand); **Mark Walters** (University of Sussex, UK)

Titles include:

Marian Duggan and Vicky Heap
ADMINISTRATING VICTIMIZATION
The Politics of Anti-Social Behaviour and Hate Crime Policy

Cato Hemmingby and Tore Bjørgo
THE DYNAMICS OF A TERRORIST TARGETING PROCESS
Anders B. Breivik and the 22 July Attacks in Norway

Irene Zempi and Neil Chakraborti
ISLAMOPHOBIA, VICTIMISATION AND THE VEIL

Palgrave Hate Studies
Series Standing Order ISBN 9781-137-49566-2 hardback
(*outside North America only*)

You can receive future titles in this series as they are published by placing a standing order. Please contact your bookseller or, in case of difficulty, write to us at the address below with your name and address, the title of the series and the ISBN quoted above.

Customer Services Department, Macmillan Distribution Ltd, Houndmills, Basingstoke, Hampshire RG21 6XS, England

palgrave▶pivot

The Dynamics of a Terrorist Targeting Process: Anders B. Breivik and the 22 July Attacks in Norway

Cato Hemmingby
Norwegian Police University College

and

Tore Bjørgo
Norwegian Police University College

DOI: 10.1057/9781137579973.0001

First published 2016 by
PALGRAVE MACMILLAN

Palgrave Macmillan in the UK is an imprint of Macmillan Publishers Limited, registered in England, company number 785998, of Houndmills, Basingstoke, Hampshire RG21 6XS.

Palgrave Macmillan in the US is a division of St Martin's Press LLC, 175 Fifth Avenue, New York, NY 10010.

Palgrave Macmillan is the global academic imprint of the above companies and has companies and representatives throughout the world.

Palgrave® and Macmillan® are registered trademarks in the United States, the United Kingdom, Europe and other countries.

ISBN: 978–1–137–57998–0 EPUB
ISBN: 978–1–137–57997–3 PDF
ISBN: 978–1–137–57996–6 Hardback

A catalogue record for this book is available from the British Library.

A catalog record for this book is available from the Library of Congress.

www.palgrave.com/pivot

DOI: 10.1057/9781137579973

Contents

Foreword

Terrorist targeting remains an issue of analytical and practical importance, and it is one to which the skills of scholarly experts can contribute in vital fashion. By focusing on one egregiously shocking episode – the Anders Behring Breivik attacks in Norway in July 2011 – Cato Hemmingby and Tore Bjørgo have produced a rigorous and significant study of one important episode, and they have done so in a manner which illuminates a much wider set of problems relating to terrorism and our responses to it.

▶ Much has been written on Breivik already. But the distinctive aspect of this book is its impressively close focus upon the operational aspects of this solo terrorist endeavour. How did Breivik set about selecting his targets, and what were the factors – long-term and more imminent – which affected this lethal process? The sources on which Hemmingby and Bjørgo draw are vivid and extensive, and they apply considerable analytical skill and contextual expertise to provide a persuasive – if sometimes distressing – set of answers to their important questions. They are open about the challenges that their sources embody, and they address these calmly and professionally.

Moreover, and significantly, they set Breivik in comparative perspective, which makes this short book of high value not merely to those with a Norwegian interest, but also to the wider community of scholars and states thinking about how best to respond to terrorism. The improvisatory aspects of Breivik's approach stand out, for example, as does his appalling empathy deficit. And – despite the things which make him, as the authors note, in some ways

DOI: 10.1057/9781137579973.0002

atypical – there are indeed wider lessons to be derived here. Not the least of them is the need for all of us to be realistic about how far and how consistently even the best, intelligence-led responses to terrorism will be able to thwart attacks.

The subject of this book is sharp-edged and important; the skills brought to it by the authors are deeply impressive; and the calmness and rigour applied to the Breivik case and its ramifications should serve as a model for other scholars in the field. I recommend the book very strongly; it deserves to be widely read.

Richard English
Director, The Handa Centre for the
Study of Terrorism and Political Violence (CSTPV)
University of St Andrews
July 2015

DOI: 10.1057/9781137579973.0002

Preface

The main purpose of this study has been to provide a thorough insight in the decision-making and target selection process of Anders Behring Breivik, who conducted what might be considered the most horrific solo terrorist atrocity seen to date. In most cases an in-depth insight on these processes is not possible due to lack of information. However, access to unique source material, combined with a willingly talking perpetrator, made it possible to study this case in unusual detail. Aware of the fact that more research was needed in this area, we therefore found that this opportunity should be utilized. It is of profound importance to get a better understanding of complex operational processes – not least for the practitioners within law enforcement and security professionals.

Even though some characteristics of the 22 July 2011 attacks in Norway and the perpetrator are atypical, there is also a substantial amount of generic insights to be extracted from this case. All terrorists operate within a framework where they control some factors, but far from all. There are always a number of known and expected variables, but also less expected constraints, and not to forget pure coincidences, luck and bad luck. This is exactly why operational phases in general are so dynamic, possibly even chaotic, and indeed so unpredictable, up until the moment the attack actually is committed against the chosen target. This is very much what we wanted to learn more about with this study.

The authors have enjoyed inspiration, assistance, contributions and views from a number of people. We

DOI: 10.1057/9781137579973.0003

want to express our thanks to Anders Snortheimsmoen, Tor-Geir Myhrer, Haavard Reksten, Anja Dalgaard-Nielsen, Morten Sørensen, Andrew O. Bennett, Fathali M. Moghaddam, Odd Einar Olsen, Envor M. Bjørgo Skårdalsmo, Monicha J. Hemmingby, Håvard Walla, Bjørn Egeland, Anders Grønli, Petter Nesser, Brynjar Lia and our colleagues at the Norwegian Police University College. Special thanks to Asbjørn Rachlew, who was able to provide us with advice and insights about the interviews with Breivik and where to find the most relevant sequences, due to his central role in the police investigative interview team. We are also grateful to sources and other individuals, home and abroad, who have to remain anonymous due to their positions, for fruitful discussions and contributions on the subject.

Cato Hemmingby, also holding a position as senior advisor in the Norwegian Government Security and Service Organization (GSSO), would like to thank Jon Ivar Mehus, for supporting the Ph.D. run at the Norwegian Police University College and the University of Stavanger from the start. Thanks also to good colleagues at GSSO: SIBE. In addition, and for different reasons, gratitude must be expressed to Irene B. Fjeller, Roar Havneraas, Tor-Inge Kristoffersen, Julia Wanda, Tore Bekkevold and Arve Edvardsen, as well as Michael and Eskil who have a busy dad. Finally, co-author, mentor and friend Tore Bjørgo deserves a few special words. Many years ago he learnt from one of the best within terrorism research, Alex P. Schmid, before he stepped up to the elite division himself. Following in his footsteps, the way he includes and guides us, and generously shares his impressive knowledge, is no less than exemplary.

Finally, we want to dedicate this book to all the 77 victims of the 22 July attacks and their affected families, and also the emergency services and the volunteers making indispensable efforts to save lives after the attacks.

DOI: 10.1057/9781137579973.0003

palgrave▶**pivot**

www.palgrave.com/pivot

1

Introduction

Abstract: *This study provides an in-depth analysis of solo terrorist Anders Behring Breivik, with focus on the target selection process and related operational aspects. In this chapter the authors explain in greater detail the objectives of this study, the need for more research in the area and the unique source material that made this project possible. There are also important ethical aspects related to studies such as this, which is addressed in this chapter.*

Keywords: decision-making; operational issues; research ethics; research need; solo terrorist; sources; target selection; terrorism

Hemmingby, Cato, and Tore Bjørgo. *The Dynamics of a Terrorist Targeting Process: Anders B. Breivik and the 22 July Attacks in Norway.* Basingstoke: Palgrave Macmillan, 2016. DOI: 10.1057/9781137579973.0004.

How do terrorists select their targets? What kind of factors and circumstances influence their decision-making? This book explores these issues by analysing one particular case of terrorism conducted by a single actor. It is based on unusually detailed information about the terrorist's reasoning and deliberations. The case in question is Anders Behring Breivik's extremely brutal and ruthless attacks on 22 July 2011 in Norway. He first detonated a vehicle-born fertilizer bomb in the centre of the Government District in downtown Oslo, before he followed up with a shooting attack on the small island Utøya, where the Labour Party's youth wing (AUF, Worker's Youth League) arranged their annual summer camp. Eight persons were killed in Oslo, while 69 people lost their lives at Utøya, including 33 victims aged less than 18 years.

The terrorist claimed to be a Justiciar Knight Commander in a network he called Knights Templar Europe. However, the following police investigation did not find any indicators or evidence that such a network actually exists.[1] Thus, he was a solo terrorist, regardless of whether we apply a narrow or broad definition (to be addressed more extensively later) of solo terrorism. Breivik also stands out as the most deadly solo terrorist we know of.

Several books have been written about Anders Behring Breivik, including a few titles that have reached the English-speaking market. These have primarily investigated his personal background and radicalization process, seeking to establish an understanding of how he turned to terrorism and was able to commit such dreadful acts.[2] Others have tried to explain his extremist acts primarily in terms of the political and ideological context he allegedly was influenced by.[3] However, there has not been the same focus on the operational aspects, which is just as important to address since the case can provide important knowledge to *practitioners* involved in law enforcement and counter-terrorism. The main objective of this book is therefore to contribute to fill the gap regarding the operational aspects, by analysing the planning and target selection process of Breivik. Here there are several important questions to address. How and why did he end up with the two target objects he finally attacked? What were the alternative targets he considered during the build-up phase? Which factors made him dismiss the targets he never attacked, and at what time in the selection process did crucial decision-making sequences take place? In most terrorist plots these questions are unlikely to be answered in detail due to unknown or dead perpetrators, lack of cooperation from terrorists captured, limited research material

DOI: 10.1057/9781137579973.0004

or no access to classified documentation that do exist. However, for the research project on which this book is based, the amount of source material and quality of sources can be characterized as far better than normal, opening for a unique opportunity to analyse the target selection process in some detail. Especially so because we here learn not just about the two targets actually attacked, but just as much from the targets he considered, but did *not* choose to attack, and why. This leaves us with a more or less complete picture, at least from the point where he started to develop concrete plans. In addition, this book puts the Norwegian perpetrator into a comparative perspective with regard to other solo terrorists, fully illustrating that he was not the typical lone wolf or solo terrorist.

Regarding primary sources the perpetrator partially wrote and partially edited the extensive compendium *2083 – A European Declaration of Independence,* under the pseudonym Andrew Berwick.[4] This 1400 page document has three parts. The first part covers the historical context, while the second part illuminates the ideology. The third part covers different operational aspects and is sometimes referred to as the military part.[5] The first two parts were predominantly cut-and-paste from other anti-Islamist authors whereas the third part, which is of greater interest regarding this book, was mainly authored by Breivik himself. Furthermore, from the moment he was captured and up to the trial, Breivik spoke willingly with the police in a series of investigative interviews. These interviews, 220 hours, were all recorded on audio and video (with the exception of the first interview after his capture, which was on audio only). The police investigative interviews with Breivik were based on the principles of free explanation in order to obtain as much factual information as possible from the suspect rather than to extract a confession. The interview procedures used by the Norwegian police are known as K.R.E.A.T.I.V., which is based on the English PEACE model.[6] This methodology has sometimes been criticized for producing too much information irrelevant to the main issue of the trial – whether the accused is guilty of the crime or not.[7] However, the investigative interviews with Anders Behring Breivik, produced data of great detail and relevance to academic research on the decision-making processes of the terrorist. Obviously proud of his terrorist attacks, Breivik explained in detail about the operational challenges and difficulties he faced in his preparations and execution of the attacks, about the adjustments he had to make to his plans, and about how he selected and discarded potential

DOI: 10.1057/9781137579973.0004

targets. This provided a unique access to the thinking and reasoning of the terrorist.

After a lengthy and complex process, the Norwegian General Attorney granted us, the authors of this book, access to all the protocolled, summarizing transcripts from police investigative interviews with the suspect, about 1200 pages, as well as the DVD recordings from these interviews related to the research topic.[8] These summaries have been analysed to identify interesting and relevant sequences, and then we watched the DVD recordings in case there were more details on these. Breivik also talked willingly during the trial, where he could make a free statement to explain his acts, as well as being subjected to heavy cross-examination. The Norwegian news agency NTB has provided accurate word-by-word transcripts[9] from the days of the trial when Breivik was examined, supplementing the official court documents. In addition, the authors have also had some correspondence by mail with Breivik, which has provided some additional input. In the writing process Breivik also agreed to be interviewed in prison, since there were a few details we wanted to get clarified, but this was cancelled by Breivik due to "other priorities". We discuss further the issue of interviewing Breivik under the section on ethical issues.

Finally, the authors have talked to different primary sources, including two security officers from the Norwegian Government Security and Service Organization (GSSO) on duty at the time of the attacks in Oslo.[10] Furthermore, we were given exclusive access to interview the team leader of the national police emergency response unit (Delta), who was leading and participating in the arrest of the terrorist on the island.[11]

Reliability and validity: can Breivik's explanations be taken as truth, and do they have any relevance beyond this case?

As mentioned earlier, Breivik's detailed explanations may provide a unique access to the thinking and reasoning of a terrorist. However, this raises some questions about the reliability and validity of the information Breivik provided to the police during the investigative interviews and to the court during the trial. It is not uncommon that suspects in criminal cases lie to the police and the court. How truthful was the information Breivik provided? And more fundamentally, was it based on reality or phantasy and delusion?

DOI: 10.1057/9781137579973.0004

The question of whether Breivik was sane or insane became a main issue during the trial and triggered a huge public debate about the psychiatric evaluation procedures in the Norwegian court system in general. Was Breivik psychotic or schizophrenic, and maybe even not eligible for punishment and imprisonment, or was he an unusually cynical and calculating terrorist?

In Chapter 7, we discuss more in detail into the issue of whether Breivik was insane or a rational actor. Here we merely summarize: Shortly after Breivik was arrested, the court appointed a forensic psychiatric evaluation team to assess whether he was sane and fit for punishment. In the conclusion of their report, made public on 29 November 2011, the two psychiatrists found him to be psychotic at the time of his criminal actions as well as during their observation after his arrest, and also as suffering from paranoid schizophrenia. When the full report was leaked to the media, there were substantial protests from fellow psychiatrists as well as from experts on right-wing extremism and terrorism, casting severe doubt about the basis for the conclusions of the psychiatric assessment. As a result, the court appointed a second psychiatric team, which reached the opposite conclusion: Breivik was not psychotic or insane, but suffered from narcissistic and dissocial personality disorders. However, both psychiatric teams agreed (although using different diagnostic terms) that he suffered from severe personality disorders. In their verdict, the court sided with the second psychiatric assessment and found Breivik sane and fit to be punished. Thus, Breivik was not a deluded or insane individual, but a ruthless and rational solo terrorist. If he had been found deluded, then an analysis of his decision-making would have been less useful.

However, that he can be considered to be sane and not deluded does not mean that his statements can be taken as truth. On some key issues in Breivik's explanations, he obviously bluffed. Shortly after he had surrendered to the police, he claimed that there were two other terrorist cell members out there, ready to strike with even more deadly consequences, and that the police could save 300 lives if they gave in for his demands.[12] These two cell members never materialized and intensive police investigation concluded that there was no evidence or indications that they existed. However, Breivik never admitted that this was a bluff. Similarly, he also stuck to the claim that the Knights Templar organization actually existed and that an alleged meeting did take place in London in 2003 where he was given his mission. He did concede during the trial that his description of the group was "pompous" in order to maximize the

DOI: 10.1057/9781137579973.0004

propaganda effect, and he played down that dimension when he realized that his preoccupations with uniforms and rituals made him appear insane. When Breivik was asked in court what he meant by his repeated use of the term "pompous", he explained:

> If you represent, let us say, a group and you want to communicate it in a way, which optimise the propaganda effect, you convey it in a pompous way. Instead of telling about four sweaty guys in a basement you use other ways to describe it.[13]

Again, the police found no evidence that such an organization ever existed, even in a less "pompous" version. However, both these rather obvious bluffs can be seen as a rational way to maximize the psychological effect of his terrorist attacks by making his one-man organization appear bigger and more dangerous than it actually was. It was also his expressed strategy to try to instigate copycat operations, hoping to turn his (phantom) organization into reality. Thus, Breivik bluffed and lied when it served his strategic purpose.

However, when it came to operational details, what he actually did and prepared, his explanations seem to be far more reliable. The police investigation found little discrepancy between his explanations and the evidence documented by the investigators. From our analytical purpose, the most problematic part was probably that when the police investigative interviewers sometimes challenged him on why he did this or that, he sometimes seemed to make up a clever reason to make it appear as he had thought about and considered everything. When challenged further, he often became increasingly vague. In reality, some of his decisions were based on very skimpy intelligence and poor hostile reconnaissance. He obviously tried to appear as a more professional terrorist than he actually was. So again, some of Breivik's explanations must be taken with a grain of salt, as possible post-rationalization.

Given these reservations, does this case offer any insights that may be of relevance beyond the specific example of the 22 July terrorist attacks in Norway? We think so, even if Breivik is not a "typical" or "representative" solo terrorist. First, this case demonstrates how terrorists – single actors as well as group-based – may have to change their plans as things often do not develop as they had intended and expected. This case shows that terrorist decision-making and target selection is a highly dynamic process. Moreover, many of the factors that constrained Breivik's operation and influenced his decision-making, such as lack of time, capacity and funding, are generic to most terrorists and may therefore provide insights which go beyond this particular case. The way he organized and prepared the whole operation, as well as how he handled operational security challenges, are also of general relevance.

Ethical issues

General principles of research ethics obviously also apply to research on terrorism and political extremism. Just because we are studying people who carry out horrific acts, we cannot forgo all ethical boundaries. However, research in this field does raise several critical issues in research ethics. One of these questions is how far the general requirement for informed consent applies when it comes to empirical research on terrorists and violent extremists? Most researchers in the field would probably say that there is obviously no such requirement to obtain informed consent from terrorists, due to the fact that they are normally inaccessible and that it does not make sense if we had to abstain from doing research on terrorists and other evil-doers, just because they refuse to cooperate and give their consent. However, some terrorists are accessible, in particular those who are imprisoned or who are otherwise no longer active. It also depends on the kind of data to be collected. Publicly available data, such as media reports and public court documents, can usually be used by researchers, without informed consent from the militant activists. However, a direct interview with an imprisoned terrorist should not and cannot be carried out without an informed consent from the interviewee. Between these two extremes there are some grey areas where obtaining informed consent may or may not be required, but it may still be useful to obtain such consent.

When we wanted to get access to the transcripts and DVD recordings of the police investigative interviews with the 22 July terrorist, Breivik, Anders Behring we knew that access to these data were strictly restricted, and that it would require permission from the General Attorney, the Council for Confidentiality and Research appointed by the Ministry of Justice and Public Security, as well as the Data Protection Official for Research. By obtaining informed consent from the research subject, Anders Behring Breivik, we assumed that this process of obtaining permission would be easier. Consequently, we wrote to Breivik in prison in October 2012, six weeks after his conviction. We informed him about our research project and all the usual rights of research subjects, and provided a form where

DOI: 10.1057/9781137579973.0004

he could select between several levels of consent, which would give us different degrees of access to data and use of data. In addition, there was an open field where he could provide a justification for his decision. Breivik checked all boxes giving consent and wrote (in his own words) that we could "to use all material in all contexts, for all time, without any restrictions". This consent certainly helped us in obtaining the necessary permissions. We got access to the transcript and relevant DVD recordings in June 2013, about eight months after our initial request. Without Breivik's informed consent, we believe the process would have been much lengthier and perhaps we might have been refused access to the data.

The data from the police investigative interviews with Breivik provided us with almost all the information we needed for our study, but there were still a few issues we would like to clarify and explore further. In January 2014 we therefore decided to contact Breivik in prison and ask for an interview. This time, his response was (apparently) far more negative:

> Why do you think I want to contribute to make the Norwegian police, and the Swedish, Danish, German, British police improving their insight into target selection and ideological, strategic and operational considerations, regarding "nationalist groups", when improved knowledge about this will reduce such groups' chance of succeeding? I assume you believe that my alleged [narcissistic] "personality traits" will make me more disposed to act against the interest of these [nationalist groups]. This is wrong.
>
> This being said, I want to communicate that I will comply with your request. [Prison] visitor form is attached. [Letter from Breivik, dated 05.02.2014)

In our previous correspondence with Breivik we had informed him in general terms about the purpose of our research project ("to understand better the processes whereby terrorist actors select their targets"), but we did not spell out the ultimate purpose of our study, which he obviously saw through. This raises the question about how far does the requirement of openness about the purpose of the research project apply in terrorism research. In our case we believe that we were sufficiently transparent about the purpose of our study, given the information we had provided, as well as being open about the fact that we both worked at the Norwegian Police University College. Breivik was also well informed about Tore Bjørgo' roles in several previous prevention initiatives (Bjørgo 1997, 2013).[14]

Despite Breivik's denial, it is hard to avoid the conclusion that he accepted to be interviewed because he, due to his narcissistic personality, craved for attention from researchers – even if it might harm his followers' chances of success in carrying out future terrorist operations. Around the same time as Breivik corresponded with us about a possible interview, he also wrote letters to several other Norwegian researchers in the field, inviting them to interview him in prison (we were informed about this by some of these colleagues). He also tried to instigate a kind of competition between these researchers about "being the first" to interview him, the famous terrorist. In some cases he enticed researchers with the possibility of getting exclusive access to new revelations.[15] In a new letter (dated 28.04.2014), he asked for political clarifications and concessions before he could accept an interview. In early May 2014 he postponed our interview as he was displeased about our (slow) response and because he now "had other priorities". We decided not to push any more for an interview since we were originally only seeking a few minor clarifications, and just as importantly, we were reluctant to play his game.

There were also other ethical concerns. It was a dilemma to break the taboo among Norwegian scholars and journalists against interviewing Breivik. Survivors and family members of Breivik's victims opposed giving him more attention. As one mother put it:

> My daughter's killer was convicted to isolation and detention. I cannot see that you can get more out of him beyond all documentation and cross-examination. Now he is changing his views and is fooling everyone to get publicity. Keep yourself too good for that! [...] If you are the first [researchers] to talk with him, what do you think you will get from that? Media publicity? Let this be my advice. [...] I hope you understand my despair and suffering in all of this.[16]

However, when we explained to her that the purpose of our research was to provide knowledge which might help to prevent future attacks, she accepted that it might be justifiable to interview the terrorist for such a specific purpose – even if it caused suffering to the victims and next of kin. It could also be added that an interview with Breivik would probably lead to a couple of footnotes in this publication, and no media coverage whatsoever.

Notes

1   Oslo District Court – Judgment 2012-08-24 TOSLO-2011-188627-24E.
2   See for example; Borchgrevink, Aage Storm (2013). *A Norwegian Tragedy: Anders Behring Breivik and the Massacre at Utøya.* Cambridge: Polity; Seierstad, Åsne (2015). *One of Us.* London: Virago.

DOI: 10.1057/9781137579973.0004

3   See for example; Bangstad, Sindre (2014). *Anders Breivik and the Rise of Islamophobia.* London: Zed Books.

4   The pseudonym used by Anders Behring Breivik in his compendium, Andrew Berwick, is categorically used in the bibliography and notes.

5   Berwick, Andrew (2011). *2083 – A European Declaration of Independence.* The page-reference here starts with the front page, which is not the case with the edition posted by Breivik 22.07.2011.

6   For details about the Norwegian police approach to investigative interviewing, see Ivar Andre Fahsing and Asbjørn Rachlew (2009). Investigative interviewing in the Nordic region. In Tom Williamson, Becky Milne & Stephen Savage (ed.) *International developments in investigative interviewing,* 39–65. Collumpton: Willan.

7   Report: Riksadvokatens arbeidsgruppe 2013: 11, 74 (unpublished report on investigative interviews from a working group for the Director of Public Prosecutions).

8   We specifically did not ask for access to DVD-sequences intruding on the privacy of "third parties". The police investigative interviews consisted of a total of 220 hours on audio/video recordings, plus a few hours audio only from the first interrogation immediately after Breivik was arrested at Utøya. Breivik himself signed and confirmed the content of each investigative police interview, in total making up 1200 pages of summarizing transcripts.

9   The NTB (word-by-word) court transcripts consisted of 463 pages.

10 Cato Hemmingby conducted these interviews in June and July 2015.

11 The national police emergency response unit, *Beredskapstroppen* (call sign Delta), is the elite counterterrorism unit in Norway, equal to SC&O19 in the UK, GIGN in France and GSG-9 in Germany. The unit is based in Oslo and covers a range of tasks, beside the CT-function. On 22 July 2011, Delta was under the command of Anders Snortheimsmoen. The current commander, from 2014 onwards, is Helge Mehus.

12 On several occasions Breivik used the expression *one-man cells*, and it is clear in the first improvised police interview at Utøya that he also tried to convince the police officers that there were two other individuals operating independently from each other; Police interview 08,01 (transcripts from the first interview of Breivik at Utøya on 22 July 2011).

13 VG Nett (2012). *Ord-for-ord, dag 43,* 17.04.2012.

14 In particular, Breivik disliked that Tore Bjørgo in 1996–97 initiated the first Exit project to facilitate disengement from racist and right-wing groups, as he (correctly) considered that this was meant to weaken these movements.

15 To counteract Breivik's manipulation, we brought up the issue of interviewing Breivik at a public meeting on research ethics and the 22 July attacks, and discussed the ways he tried to play researchers out against each other, as well

DOI: 10.1057/9781137579973.0004

as other ethical dilemmas. https://www.etikkom.no/Aktuelt/Nyheter/2014/ Forskere-vil-intervjue-Behring-Breivik/

16 This SMS exchange from April 2014 is cited with permission from the mother of a girl (age 18), killed at Utøya on 22 July 2011.

DOI: 10.1057/9781137579973.0004

2
Theoretical Perspectives and Methodological Approaches

Abstract: *Terrorist target selection processes may be profoundly complex and dynamic, affected by a considerable number of different of variables. Hence, a solid theoretical and methodological approach is important. This study has used a generic typology as a starting point for structuring variables found, and applied case study process tracing in order to establish when decisions related to the target selection have been made, and even more importantly, to find the reasons for the choices made.*

Keywords: case study; external factors; ideology; interaction; internal factors; methodology; process tracing; strategy; theory; typology; unpredictability

Hemmingby, Cato, and Tore Bjørgo. *The Dynamics of a Terrorist Targeting Process: Anders B. Breivik and the 22 July Attacks in Norway.* Basingstoke: Palgrave Macmillan, 2016. DOI: 10.1057/9781137579973.0005.

DOI: 10.1057/9781137579973.0005

Qualitative, in-depth terrorism research is challenging due to the fact that the persons involved are part of clandestine and autonomous social environments, and not to forget, involved in subversive and criminal activity. Traditional ethnographic methods such as fieldwork and direct observation is usually not an option, and in most cases interviewing the violent actors involved is not possible – at least when it comes to terrorists still active.[1] Therefore, case study research based on within-case process-tracing, and if applicable or relevant, cross-case comparison, stands out as a sensible approach. Furthermore, this is described as a powerful way to create middle-range theories that are consistent with both the historical explanations of individual cases and the general theoretical patterns evident across cases" (George & Bennett 2005:149).

This particular case is part of a larger on-going project on terrorist target selection processes.[2] A typology has been developed, and as such it represents a starting point for typological theorizing. What we may characterize as the structured target selection process starts when the actor in question seriously considers, or takes a decision, to actually commit a terrorist attack. In the other end, the process culminates with an attack, or attempt of such, on the selected target(s). Hence, the decision to conduct an attack and the attack itself represent the two dependent variables in a target selection process. Between the start and end of this journey there are multiple independent variables affecting the target selection. Here these independent variables are sorted into four main categories. On the upper level, from this point called the strategic level, the categories of *ideology* and *strategy* constitute the major framework for a terrorist actor. On the tactical level, the categories of *internal factors* and *external factors* represent the operational capacities and constraints the actor must take into consideration. Within each of these four categories an unknown number of explanatory variables may appear.

This typology is first and foremost a tool for structured identification and sorting of variables with an impact on the target selection process, but identification and sorting alone are not enough. It is just as essential to disclose how these independent variables interact with each other, to find the answers to *why* the terrorist(s) decides on this and not that, which is vital in order to understand the processes. Obviously, a target selection process may often be profoundly complicated, dynamic, maybe unstructured or even partially chaotic, and accordingly, a challenge to clarify. This just underlines the need for a structured and holistic

DOI: 10.1057/9781137579973.0005

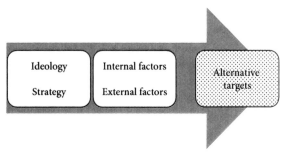

FIGURE 2.1   *Typology for target selection processes*
Source: Cato Hemmingby.

approach, if the objective is to establish the *ratio decidendi* behind the decisions made.

This generic typology for target selection processes lays the foundation of a combined deductive and inductive development of typological theory. The skeleton of the model regarding the sorting of independent variables is partially based on the work done by Drake in the 1990s (Drake 1998: 76). However, some adjustments have been made, both regarding terms used and the increased focus interaction and dynamics.

Ideology and strategy represent the major framework

Information we retrieve relating to ideology and strategy will provide us with the major framework terrorists operate within. This may in fact be all we know about actors in an early phase of their existence, and not to forget, most terrorist groups and cells are relatively short-lived.[3]

Ideology will supply us with the set of beliefs and moral reflections that constitute the basic fundament of the actor's rationality.[4] Accordingly, we here expect to gain knowledge about the actor's subjective world-view, the current and futuristic threat-picture, who the identified enemies are, more detailed characterizations of these enemies, moral justifications and legitimacy for violent actions, as well as the ultimate objectives. Though some of these variables can be rather straightforward to register from the outside, there may also be interesting internal discussions within groups and movements, and also their potential supporters. Moral justification for acting against some specific parts of the public,

DOI: 10.1057/9781137579973.0005

and legitimacy for extraordinary brutal violence are just two issues that may create discontent within terrorist organizations. For example, is it justifiable to target civilians who are not a part in the armed conflict? Is it acceptable to kill women and children? Is it legitimate to attack people with the same religious beliefs who are not cooperating with the enemy? Such targeted-related questions have fractionated a number of groups and movements.

Strategy in our context is often about how an armed conflict is to be won for political purposes (Mahnken 2010). Put very short, strategies are long-term plans on how to achieve long-term goals. Strategic objectives of terrorists, also with impact on the choice of targets, may be sorted into the six categories of *compliance, advertisement, endorsement, provocation, societal disruption and threat elimination.*[5] By compliance we mean the change the terrorists seek to achieve from the psychological target. Attacks are to generate advertisement for the cause through maximum media attention. Through endorsement the movement want to consolidate their ideological foundation and general support among followers, potential recruits and outsiders. Through attacks of provocation the authorities may in rashness initiate operations that will prove counterproductive and benefit the terrorists. By societal disruption the attackers seek to affect the everyday life of a society over time, in order to boost a public mistrust against the authorities – ultimately increasing the political pressure. Finally, threat elimination covers a range of issues, from taking care of internal security and reducing enemy capacity, to maintaining the strength of the movement towards competing actors and unwanted processes. As such spoiling and outbidding are included in this category.

Large actors may use different strategies in order to achieve specific objectives and they also might adjust their strategies over time. However, solo terrorists and small-group actors will most often have to rely on a simple, straightforward strategy. They will often choose between one-offs and series of attacks, and must also consider the frequency of attacks. In addition, there are operational issues and decisions that may have strategic importance – much due to the tremendous difference they potentially may lead to regarding possibilities, results and reactions in the aftermath – both internally and externally. Major decisions are for example linked to issues such as area of operations (local, regional or global), indiscriminate versus selective killing, mass-casualties versus low-casualties and suicide actions versus escape or capture. Several

DOI: 10.1057/9781137579973.0005

terrorist groups, networks and organizations have experienced serious backfire after major terrorist operations – both successful and failed attacks included.

The tactical level: internal and external factors

On the tactical level terrorists' scope for action is affected by internal and external factors. Internal factors are variables the actors themselves possess and/or have the possibility to control. The external factors are variables the terrorists do not control, but still must (if known) take into consideration. Furthermore, there may also at any time surface operational factors that are not foreseen, such as pure coincidences.

Subgroups of variables within the category of internal factors are for example the actor's manpower, know-how and skills, weapons and equipment, intelligence gathering ability, funding and network of contacts. We must here also include personal and psychological dimensions, including intragroup dynamics if applicable, because, what goes on inside the head of the terrorists? It is known that in the case of solo terrorists, personality disorders and other mental disturbances are quite common.[6] This may for example influence the degree of discrimination and brutality in the targeting. Furthermore, intragroup processes may have an impact when terrorists discuss what or who to target. Is it room for discussion and individual opinions at all, and what are the dynamics in play with regard to strong leaders and followers? Furthermore, within a network or a fairly structured organization the leadership's discourse, as well as the dialogue between the leadership and those carrying out the attack, is relevant. Sometimes it can be questioned whether the discourse from central leaders in a remote location, is followed in practice on the ground level in other parts of the world. Is for example the targeting as indiscriminate, as the rhetoric from spiritual and ideological leaders suggests?

Regarding the external factors and the freedom to act, terrorists must relate themselves to international and domestic security arrangements and countermeasures. Equally so, the local conditions in the area of operations and the level of security at attractive target objects do affect them. However, even though external factors will represent constraints for terrorists, there are always opportunities left to be exploited, and most terrorists will in the end of a process have several targets to choose from.

The tactical level, where capacities and opportunities are weighed against each other, is normally particularly challenging to establish and analyse. One factor is the need for detailed information, but it is also a fact that the number of potential variables at this level may be very high. They also vary with regard to nature and shape, increasing the analytical challenges. As described before, the actor in question will control some of these variables, and others not. Therefore, as an operation is set in motion, it becomes evident that even the most resourceful and ruthless terrorists act under a number of constraints that affect the scope for action. Also important to note, even seemingly trivial matters may have profound influence at any stage in the process.

A dynamic process: the challenge of interaction

Recognizing the fact that the independent variables from the four main categories are not living separate lives, but affect each other in a dynamic process, *interaction* is a keyword. Ideally, a target should be in accordance with all kinds of preferences the actor may have, but how often is that the case? Probably not very often, and it is more likely that pre-set plans and priorities are disturbed, bringing compromises and pragmatism into the dynamic target selection process. In general, unexpected changes are making it more difficult not only for the terrorists, but also for the analysts on the other side. Importantly, it must also be acknowledged that targeting processes are not homogenous. Although we have seen a number of large, well-prepared, seemingly linear and structured terrorist operations through modern history, these are probably outnumbered by far by operations that best may be characterized as poorly planned, chaotic and marked by hasty decision-making – while a lot of operations are somewhere in between.[7]

Regardless of how structured a process has been, terrorists will normally have several targets to choose from, if they have not been locked on a specific target from the start. They then enter the final decision-making phase, where minor details and situational circumstances may prove decisive. Even as an operation is initiated, targets may change in the last moment for different reasons.

As described earlier, the dynamic target selection process is affected by a high number of different variables, further complicated by interaction. A reduced focus on some type of variables or certain parts of

DOI: 10.1057/9781137579973.0005

the targeting process will inevitably construct problematic trade-offs. Therefore, if the main objective is to achieve a complete overview of a target selection process, we need to bring in all the relevant variables, as well as the interaction part, even though it is certainly making the research more complex and challenging.

Notes

1   This does not necessarily mean that field research and interviews are impossible in terrorism research. See Dolnik, Adam (2011). Conducting Field Research on Terrorism: A Brief Primer. *Perspectives on Terrorism*, Vol. 5, No. 2.

2   Cato Hemmingby's ph.d. project on target selection consists of three case studies. In addition to the case of Anders Behring Breivik, he analyses the targeting practice of militant Islamist in Western Europe for the last 20 years, and the Provisional Irish Republican Army from 1970 to 1998.

3   Jongman, Albert J. (2011). Introduction to the world directory of extremist, terrorist and other organisations associated with guerilla warfare, political violence, protest, organised crime and cyber-crime. In Schmid, Alex P. (ed) *The Routledge Handbook of Terrorism Research*. London: Routledge, 341; Hutchinson, Steven & O'Malley, Pat (2007), *How terrorist groups decline*, ITAC Volume 2007–1, http://www.itac.gc.ca/pblctns/tc_prsnts/2007-1-eng.asp, retrieved 12.01.2014.

4   Ideology derives from the Greek terms *idea* and *logos*. Concise Oxford English Dictionary, 11th edition (2006): p.707

5   Adapted from different sources: See Thornton, Terror as a weapon of political agitation in Eckstein, ed. (1965) *Internal War*. New York: The Free Press of Glencoe; Hutchinson, Martha Crenshaw (1978). *Revolutionary Terrorism: The FLN in Algeria, 1954–1962*. Stanford: Hoover Institution Press; Drake (1998); Kydd and Walter (2006). The Strategies of Terrorism, *International Security*, Vol. 31, No. 1 (Summer 2006), 49–80.

6   See for example, COT report (2007). *Lone-Wolf Terrorism*; Hewitt, Christopher (2003). *Understanding Terrorism in America*. London: Routledge; Spaaij, Ramon (2012): *Understanding Lone Wolf Terrorism*. London: Springer; Gill, Paul (2015). *Lone-Actor Terrorists: A Behavioural Analysis*. Oxon: Routledge.

7   See for example the interesting publication; Schuurman, Bart & Eijkman, Quirine (2015). *Indicators of terrorist intent and capability: Tools for threat assessment*. Dynamics of Asymmetric Conflict: Pathways toward terrorism and genocide, http//dx.doi.org/10.1080/17467586.2015.1040426

DOI: 10.1057/9781137579973.0005

3
The Target Overview Dataset

Abstract: *Thorough analysis of police investigative interviews, detailed court transcripts and other documents have resulted in an overview of persons, objects and events that potentially could represent attractive targets for Anders Behring Breivik. These are categorized into four levels. Most importantly this chapter illustrates what the perpetrator did not choose to prioritize, and the reasons for these are illuminated. For Breivik, symbolism, shock effect and maximum attention was paramount.*

▶

Keywords: court transcripts; data set; decision-making; iconic; manifesto; overview; police investigative interviews; selection; symbolic; target categories; targets

Hemmingby, Cato, and Tore Bjørgo. *The Dynamics of a Terrorist Targeting Process: Anders B. Breivik and the 22 July Attacks in Norway.* Basingstoke: Palgrave Macmillan, 2016. DOI: 10.1057/9781137579973.0006.

The following target overview dataset illustrates potential target objects in Anders Behring Breivik's case. It is based on a thorough examination of all police investigative interviews and accurate court transcriptions, and all potential target objects were registered. More precisely, each object listed has been mentioned or more thoroughly discussed by the terrorist on one or more occasions, and this in a context implying that from Breivik's point of view they had features that made them potentially attractive as targets. It is important to underline that most of these objects listed were not part of concrete attack plans, but obviously each and every one of them has attracted his attention at one time or another. Hence, it is of interest to establish the reasons why those target objects not included in plans were discarded. As explained in more detail later, most potential target objects were to be dismissed because they simply were not important or symbolic enough. However, the overview also reveals target objects the terrorist could have been seriously interested in, if he had possessed greater capacity, for example more manpower. Furthermore, it provides us with valuable information regarding the *type of targets* that attracted the attention and interest from Breivik's part. Following this, it has a value as we consider the attractiveness of symbolic and iconic targets in general. However, most importantly, it illustrates how the selection process narrows down towards the final targets actually attacked in this particular case. Since Breivik in his compendium names a broad range of enemies and potential targets, it must be emphasized that this target overview is limited to his operation 22 July 2011 in some way, and not the general thoughts in his compendium.

In total the target overview lists 65 objects. Three objects that for different reasons could be mistaken for potential target objects have been left out of the total list.[1] Equally important to note, some objects on the list are in reality consisting of a number of objects. For example, Breivik refers to the *asylum lobby,* which is a collective term he used on all NGOs working for the rights of asylum-seekers and immigrants to Norway. In addition, EU- and UN-buildings outside Norway represent a significant number of possible buildings to strike against. Hence, the number of 65 targets in total is in reality a modest estimate regarding what the perpetrator could have established an interest for in a targeting context.

The listed target objects are sorted in four levels, where the target objects have been placed after the proven interest of the perpetrator. The terrorist's assumed capacity has also been a consideration regarding a few objects. The levels are respectively coded from Level (L) 1 to 4, and they are in the following part presented and dealt with in the reverse order, illustrating how it narrows down towards the 22 July attacks. Level 4 consists of objects that are assessed to be highly hypothetical. In general, most of them can only be regarded as wish-full thinking from Breivik's side, and they are clearly unrealistic when his capacity is taken into consideration. Some of the objects in Level 4 were also not attractive due to the context and the situation at the time. Level 3 includes potential targets that would have been within the perpetrator's capacity, but at large it is clear that they have not been seriously considered. If any targeting reflections at all, they have been clearly superficial and without any sign of follow-up. Level 2 includes target objects that have been under serious consideration. All of them can be related to concrete ideas, and most of them also to planning or preparation. Level 1 consists of the two objects actually attacked on 22 July 2011.

The listed objects were sorted after the *type of targets* they represented into seven *target categories* (TC). Note that these categories are not generic, in the sense that they are appropriate for use in any case, but customized for this particular case. Here we make a distinction among *Government and authorities (TC1), Economic/infrastructure (TC2), Events (TC3), Law enforcement / military /security apparatus (TC4), NGOs (TC5), Media (TC6)* and *Others (TC7)*. In TC1 both state and municipality bodies are included, and also politicians and members of the royal family. Some target objects could obviously cross into two categories, such as a political event on a ferry or at a public square, but here it is nevertheless chosen to keep events in a category of its own. This is because some specific features related to events, such as shifting locations and a limited time frame, make such targets in many ways different from static objects, such as buildings. In general, the events considered by Breivik were either linked to his political opponents or the news media. The total overview in Breivik's case is depicted in Figure 3.1.

From the total overview with 65 listed objects, nine of them remain at Level 4. Offshore oil and gas installations, on-shore gas installations and nuclear facilities in Norway (research and test facilities) and Sweden are placed at this level due to the obvious lacking capacity of a single perpetrator coming from the outside. Regarding the oil and gas installations, Breivik has stated that the Norwegian state is immune to economic attacks due to the solid financial situation of the country (Police interviews 08,09,01; 08,29,01). Therefore he did not see much

DOI: 10.1057/9781137579973.0006

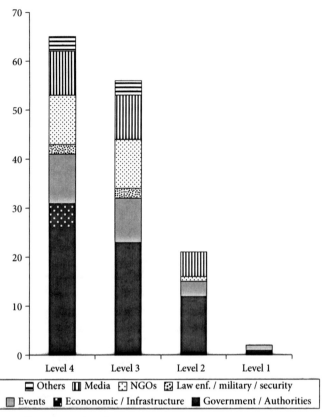

FIGURE 3.1   *Target overview data set*
Source: Cato Hemmingby.

point in initiating an operation with economical damage as the main objective. A bomb attack on the ferry between Norway and Denmark is also assessed to be a highly unlikely alternative. Not necessarily due to his capacity, as getting a vehicle loaded with explosives on board a ferry is fully possible, but first and foremost with regard to the *civilian loss factor* he has claimed to take into consideration in the target selection process (Police interviews 08,01; 08,03,01; 08,08,01; 08,26,01; NTB court transcripts 19.04.2012; 20.04.2012). Furthermore, the idea itself also seems to be a hypothetical thought surfacing during a police interview, and there are absolutely no indications that Breivik considered such an attack. EU- and UN-buildings outside Norway are also assessed to be Level 4 objects, due to the fact that Breivik was never interested in conducting

DOI: 10.1057/9781137579973.0006

operations abroad. He wrote about such targets in his compendium, but in his own target selection process these were never an alternative (Police interview 08,29,01). It is also highly questionable whether Breivik possessed the necessary capacity needed for such attacks abroad. For one, high-symbolic EU- and UN-objects are in general rather well protected, and the Norwegian terrorist would be operating away from his home ground. For a solo terrorist determined not to involve others for operational reasons, it would prove particularly difficult. No one could then compensate for his lack of local knowledge, and he could not have established such a thorough cover for letting a farm and getting fertilizer as he did in Norway. Finally, to try to assassinate President Obama during the Nobel peace prize ceremony in Oslo City Hall in 2009 was in a police investigative interview dismissed by Breivik himself as beyond his capacity (Police interview 08,29,01). Beside the fact that it would be impossible due to the extensive security arrangements in place, the event also took place too early in Breivik's process, as he was not by far ready to act at the time of president Obama's visit to the Norwegian capital.

Potential target objects with limited symbolic value

After placing nine objects in Level 4 we are left with 56 potential target objects overall, and 35 of these objects constitute Level 3. All of these 35 objects are considered to be legitimate targets from the perpetrator's point of view. In addition, they were all within the terrorist's operational capacity. In fact, it is more likely than not that an attack on any of these target objects would have been fatal for those struck. However, just as with Level 4, we must in Level 3 beware of the possibility that some objects may have come up rather coincidentally, for example as more or less instant ideas or loose remarks during the police interviews.

The 35 objects in Level 3 have three common features. First, they have all attracted Breivik's attention for some reason during the years before the attack. Second, he obviously disliked these objects so much that they came easy to mind when he was questioned by police. Third, they were obviously not considered to be of such importance that they qualified for direct targeting. After all, these were not particularly prestigious or influential objects, compared with most of those objects he actually took into the planning process. In other words, they were not adequately attractive regarding symbolism[2], and the potential for a "spectacular"

DOI: 10.1057/9781137579973.0006

with massive and long-lasting media attraction would also to a lesser degree be present. High-symbolic targets and maximum media potential were two essential criterions for this terrorist.

Looking closer at the 35 objects in Level 3, there were ten politicians (potentially also including family members), nine NGO's, five event venues, four media objects, two individuals from the law enforcement sector, two education institutions, one individual from academia, one public café in the Labour Party building and the Ministry of Foreign Affairs.

Concerning the ten politicians in Level 3, it should be noted that not only representatives from the Labour Party are found. Former Prime Minister Kåre Willoch from the Conservative Party is listed, together with former Prime Minister Kjell Magne Bondevik and former Minister of Foreign Affairs Knut Wollebæk, both from the Christian Democrats. In addition, party leader and Member of Parliament Trine Schei Grande from the Social Liberal Party, who previously was in a government coalition with the Christian Democrats and the Conservative Party, is listed in Level 3.

It is clear that Norway's support of NATO's decision to bomb Serbia in 1999 frustrated Breivik significantly, and this was a direct reason for his dissatisfaction with both Bondevik and Wollebæk. Moreover, the Norwegian government's comments and reactions to the Mohammed cartoon publications from 2005, the Nobel Peace Prize to Yassir Arafat in 1994 and the immigration policies in general were upsetting the terrorist significantly (Berwick 2011: 1381; NTB court transcripts 17.04.2012; Police interviews 08,16,01; 08,20,01; 08,31,01). Still, Breivik wanted to concentrate his efforts on just one party due to his limited capacity, and that would have to be the Labour Party (Police interview 08,06,01). Labour Party politicians that drew Breivik's attention, but seemingly not important enough to become potential targets in concrete plans, were ministers Trond Giske and Anniken Huitfeldt, deputy party leader Helga Pedersen, general secretary Raymond Johansen and Member of Parliament Martin Kolberg.

The nine NGOs that are listed as potential targets in Level 3 are mainly consisting of immigrant-friendly or far-left organizations. Breivik used the expression *the asylum lobby* as a common term for several of the immigrant-friendly organizations, and here he included SOS Racism, the so-called Blitz anarchists, Norwegian Centre against Racism, as well as Amnesty International. In addition, the Norwegian terrorist declared

DOI: 10.1057/9781137579973.0006

his dislike for the NGOs Attack Norway, the Norwegian Confederation of Trade Unions (LO), the Union of Municipal and General Employees (Fagforbundet), a council in the Norwegian Church that he probably mistook for a cross-religious council and the Norwegian broadcasting board. None of these can, in the context of terrorism, be regarded as significant symbolic target objects in terms of size or political influence.

Regarding the event venues, it is important to note that Breivik would not have struck just any event indiscriminately. Also here it would be necessary that the event attracted those he regarded as enemies, such as political opponents, people from the news media or what he described as Cultural-Marxists. That could mean everything from conventions held at hotels to rallies at squares in downtown Oslo. However, it is not likely that he then would plan an attack against the most prime event venues such as Telenor Arena and Oslo Spektrum, or the Karl Johan high street of Oslo, since these venues never are used by what he considered to be enemies. On the other hand, the annual May 1st workers' day parade at Youngstorget Square or a suitable event at the House of Literature could be more likely targets for the terrorist.

The only two law enforcement individuals mentioned by Breivik in negative terms in the police investigative interviews were former National Police Commissioner Ingelin Killengreen, and the head of the Norwegian police security service (PST) until 2012, Janne Kristiansen. It is apparent that these two women in top positions had been frustrating Breivik over time, but they were nevertheless not attractive targets on Breivik's part. The terrorist has on several occasions stated that he considers the police and armed forces as potential allies needed in the struggle, and therefore potential target objects in these two sectors were never taken into any plans (Police interview 08,35; NTB court transcripts 20.04.2012). As for the cafe *Internasjonalen,* on street level in the Labour Party's HQ building, Breivik had yet again an incorrect view. He obviously thought that it was linked to the Labour Party since it was in the same building, but it was in fact a commercial and apolitical place, probably choosing their name because of their surroundings. Finally, it can be mentioned that Breivik also talked about a few individuals or institutions that seemed to come up more or less spontaneous, such as an academic at the University of Oslo and a university college at Volda, particularly known for their media study programs.

Overall, some general views and priorities on Breivik's part, combined with the fact that the potential target objects in Level 3 cannot be

DOI: 10.1057/9781137579973.0006

characterized as high-symbolic targets, held these objects away from any concrete plans Breivik made. In other words, the shift from Level 3 to the upcoming Level 2 is the significant shift, as we here leave 35 more potential target objects never seriously considered, or at least vaguely documented, and proceed to those objects that actually were included in concrete ideas and plans from Breivik's part.

Narrowing down to the actual targets

Level 2 contains the 21 objects that Breivik actually considered in different plans and some more seriously than others. One important thing to note here is that single individuals were not a priority to Breivik as main targets. He considered the overall shock-effect and the potential for advertisement of attacking one person only would be limited, in comparison to attacks of a larger scale. Hence, the politicians and others here were regarded as potential bonuses (Police interview 08,01; NTB court transcripts 19.04.2012). To briefly mention the politicians who actually could get struck by the terrorist as a so-called bonus, Prime Minister Jens Stoltenberg is a natural start. His well-protected office was on 16th floor in the H-building in the Government District, but it was facing against the Akersgata street, and not the Grubbegata street where Breivik parked his rented Volkswagen Crafter. In contrast, the office belonging to the Minister of Justice and Police Knut Storberget, on 7th floor in the same building, faced Grubbegata. This office also had quite robust protection specifications and took the blast in a satisfactory manner, as can be seen on pictures of the building after the detonation. Neither the prime minister nor the minister of justice and police were in their offices in the Government District at the time of the explosion. Breivik did not have an overview of their whereabouts at the time, but that was not his priority either, as he ultimately wanted the building to collapse.

Regarding other individuals, journalist Marte Michelet from the newspaper Dagbladet, Minister of Foreign Affairs Jonas Gahr Støre and former Prime Minister Gro Harlem Brundtland, were booked as guest speakers for different days at Utøya, and as such they were also potential "bonuses" for Breivik (Police interview 08,03,01). Rightly so, Breivik did initiate certain preparations to target these individuals at Utøya, and especially Gro Harlem Brundtland as she was the guest on the Friday

DOI: 10.1057/9781137579973.0006

Breivik eventually decided to strike. Killing her would undoubtedly have been a significant bonus in the eyes of the perpetrator, owing to her unique position in the Labour party. However, killing AUF youth camp-participants was seemingly still the main priority for Breivik at Utøya, and here we return to the previously mentioned fact. Assassination of individuals could never be a priority, as it was not spectacular or disastrous enough for the narcissistic Norwegian terrorist. It was therefore in reality 16 prioritized target objects left in Level 2, which he focused on in his planning process.

The H-building in the Government District, the Royal Palace, Oslo City Hall, the Parliament, the Parliament District, the Directorate of Immigration, the Labour Party HQ building and the office of the Socialist Left Party are all TC1 targets. The SKUP Media conference, the Labour Party's annual convention and the Labour Party Youth Camp at Utøya are TC3 targets. The only TC5 object is the Blitz Anarchist house. TC6 is represented with the newspapers VG, Dagsavisen, Aftenposten and the Norwegian broadcasting company NRK. In the end, the H-building of the Government District and the Labour Party Youth Camp at Utøya ended up in Level 1 as the final targets that Breivik actually attacked.

A detailed insight on how the concrete planning and preparation process developed regarding the Level 2 and Level 1 target objects is covered in the next chapter. Let us just here conclude that a high number of potential targets objects could be selected, but just a limited number were seriously considered. Some objects were never considered due to the obvious lack of capacity in a solo terrorist perspective, but even more apparent, a range of limited value, easily accessible, unprotected potential targets were simply not important enough for a narcissistic terrorist pursuing a spectacular operation. Hence, even though all targets may be considered symbolic to a lesser or more substantial degree, well-known and high-value symbolic targets were preferred. For his bombs we can in fact state that *iconic* buildings were especially attractive for the solo terrorist. As for the shooting attack objects, he preferred time-fixed events gathering a high number of participants within his declared enemy categories. This was more in accordance with his mass casualty focus than office buildings, where Breivik displayed an uncertainty with regard to casualty-potential and mobility opportunities inside. In total, political targets, NGOs and the media stood out as the most attractive targeting categories, and although Breivik had a special obsession with the Labour party, media ranked second.

DOI: 10.1057/9781137579973.0006

In a letter from his prison cell dated 29 September 2013,[3] Breivik specifically stated that "22/7 was mainly directed at the Labour Party and the Norwegian press". In reality, however, he did not end up attacking any media targets (even though he first planned for a shooting attack against the SKUP-conference).

Notes

1 These objects are Gunerius shopping mall, a Swedish nuclear waste facility and an individual by the name Ronny Johnsen. The latter was a Norwegian former Manchester United player that Breivik most likely mistook for Labour Party secretary Raymond Johansen. The Gunerius shopping mall has been named as a target in media and in one police interview, but closer examination have clarified that the mall's parking facilities was to be a transit place for switching cars (Dagbladet 05.05.12 *Breivik la plan om å arrangere fest for muslimer i Oslo Spektrum*, www.db.no; Police interviews 08,02; 08,03,01; ref nr 11762579).

2 Regarding terrorism and symbolism, see for example, Matusitz, Jonathan (2015). *Symbolism in Terrorism: Motivation, Communication and Behavior*. London: Rowman & Littlefield.

3 Breivik's letter was a complaint against Ila Prison and a named warden, the prison authorities and a number of institutions in the criminal justice sector, complaining that he was the victim of "the most severe case of torture in post-war northern-Europe". We received a copy of the letter directly from Breivik.

4
Anders B. Breivik's Targeting Process

Abstract: *Here Anders Behring Breivik's concrete ideas and plans are thoroughly addressed, providing more details on decision-making regarding the target objects from the two last levels in the data set overview. The typology introduced in Chapter 2 is used to shed light on the framework the terrorist operated within, and also the societal context in Norway at the time.*

Keywords: decision-making; external factors; ideology; interaction; internal factors; plans: political negligence; societal context; societal security; strategy; typology

Hemmingby, Cato, and Tore Bjørgo. *The Dynamics of a Terrorist Targeting Process: Anders B. Breivik and the 22 July Attacks in Norway.* Basingstoke: Palgrave Macmillan, 2016. DOI: 10.1057/9781137579973.0007.

It is not for this study to address or analyse Breivik's radicalization process, but a short glance at his background is still useful for the context. Anders Behring Breivik was born in 1979 in Oslo, but his parents divorced shortly after, and he grew up with his mother and a six-year older half-sister. The living conditions were reportedly unstable in the early years, and a psychological observation of him reported some worrying issues regarding the boy and his relationship with his mother. A recommendation from a centre for child and youth psychiatry that he should be transferred to a foster home at the age of four was overturned by a court decision, and a new and less alarming child welfare report.[1] Thus, the boy stayed with his mother and altogether he functioned normally and reasonably well in school, and also socially. At the age of 15, he was arrested in December 1994 in relation to spray-paint graffiti, but apart from this incident he was never involved with the police. He tried very hard to become accepted in a graffiti group, predominately consisting of youths with an immigrant (and Muslim) background. However, he was rejected as a "wannabe", and his immigrant mates also let him down in the process.

Interestingly, it was at this age he became increasingly politically conscious.[2] Breivik dropped out of upper secondary school during the third year in 1997. He wanted to go into business without further delay, and the ambitious youth was eager to make a lot of money.[3] His political interest became even stronger with time and in 1999 he became an active member of the right-wing populist Progress Party (Frp) and its youth organization (FpU).[4] This cannot be rated as an extremist party, but it is also clear that their strong anti-immigration views attracted quite a lot of voters who considered this to be a very important issue. His friends stated that he at this time expressed strong and peculiar political views.[5]

After more or less unsuccessful legal business experiences, Breivik started selling fake university diplomas, and here he made quite a lot of money. He earned as much as USD 678,000 from 2002 to 2006, only disturbed by some less fortunate investments on the stock market.[6] In the meantime Breivik failed to be included on his party's list of candidates for the municipal election in Oslo, which made him disillusioned with organized politics. His activity in the Progress party came to a halt. He claimed that he was finding the party too moderate, but the fact that his political career failed was probably the main reason for his disillusionment with regular politics. This far, Breivik's young life had been characterized by a series of failures and disappointments.[7]

DOI: 10.1057/9781137579973.0007

In 2006 Breivik moved back to his mother's flat again, and now he temporarily isolated himself from his friend, and dedicated a year to playing World of Warcraft. In the sentencing the court explained this turning point as a result of a complex process, and concluded that he had been strongly goal-oriented and structured from 2006 and until the terrorist acts in 2011.[8] The police investigation also found little to indicate that Breivik actually planned to commit a terrorist attack before 2006. As such it is likely that the build-up to the terrorist attacks in reality started in 2006–07, since he then also started to work on his compendium.[9] The first parts of his compendium, compiled and written during the early stages of his seclusion, were markedly less extreme in tenor and rhetoric than the latter parts, where he increasingly embraced a terrorist strategy. Thus, his radicalization was gradual. However, from some point during this process he became, to borrow the expression of psychiatrist Rosenqvist, *a man with a mission*.[10] However, to what extent was his "mission" and target selection influenced by his ideology?

A personalized and customized ideology

Like other solo terrorists before him, Anders Behring Breivik constructed and adhered to a personalized and customized ideology.[11] A substantial part is coherent with traditional right-wing views and rationality. However, right-wing extremism is not a fixed and one-dimensional ideology, but a rather broad range of ideologies with partly significant differences. Still, they do often have some basic characteristics in common, and the following seems to fit Breivik's perceptions of the world (Bjørgo 1997: 53–71, 272–311). A basic component in a right-wing extremist worldview is the idea that people are fundamentally different and that they are given different value, due to race, culture, religion, nationality or sexual preferences determining their basic character. For example, Breivik claimed that Muslims everywhere and at all times first and foremost will be jihadists, whose goal it is to conquer and subdue Christian Europeans (Berwick 2011: 524–27). Another typical trait of right-wing extremism is a conspiratorial view of the world, often claiming that an external enemy (e.g., Jews or Muslims) assisted by internal traitors, will take control of the society. One typical anti-Semitic variety of this rhetoric, popular among neo-Nazis, is the idea of the existence of a Zionist Occupation Government (ZOG).[12] The internal enemy will typically be identified as the authorities, political

DOI: 10.1057/9781137579973.0007

leftists, journalists, teachers and the cultural elite – what Breivik prefers to interchangeably call *Cultural Marxists* or *Multiculturalists*. In his compendium, Breivik states that the European governments have launched a great "campaign of deception" against their own people, in order to implement multiculturalism, ultimately leading to Eurabia, with the Muslims taking over Europe (Berwick 2011: 47). The system-hostility is apparent and as the blogger Peder Are Nøstvold Jensen (aka *Fjordman*) is referred to stating, *the EU must die, or Europe will die* (Berwick 2011: 330). Other issues discussed are the Islamic takeover, focus on the relative proportion of Muslims compared with non-Muslims. In his compendium, Breivik also states that he has never observed a successfully implementation of assimilation policy (Berwick 2011: 496).

Ultimately, the right-wing extremists tend to draw a picture that the race, nation or society, as we know it, will be destroyed or exterminated in this globalized world, where big changes take place rapidly.[13] They fear the risk of social deprivation, both for themselves and for the future generations. In the radicalization phase a strong *us-versus-them* attitude typically surfaces, as for most violent extremists (Moghaddam 2006: 97–98). Furthermore, Breivik expresses typical extremist feelings of group victimization, like that nationalists are being ridiculed, silenced and persecuted and that he represents the resistance (Berwick 2011: 13).

Often nationalists are ultimately focused on the local, regional and national context and situation within the borders of their country, although cross-border cooperation between far-right movements certainly always has been present to some degree. However, Breivik revealed a substantial interest for the European continent as a whole, and he has applied a rhetoric that bears strong resemblance to the way militant Islamists are talking about the establishment of an *ummah*. Hence, he was aiming for not only a pronounced national position, but just as much international recognition and status, and this through aggression towards the classical right-wing target groups, namely the Muslims and the alleged internal traitors. Breivik felt like many other solo terrorists before him that he was acting on the behalf of a majority that was unaware, unwilling or unable to do act themselves, and he subsequently expected endorsement and gratitude from masses of followers.[14]

Interestingly, the ideological views Breivik put into his compendium are controversial and hardly acceptable for some of the major far-right movements. First, he distanced himself from National Socialism, on several occasions claiming to present an alternative to this ideology, which he has characterized as an ideology of hatred, alongside multiculturalism and Islam (Police interviews 08,06,01; 08,13,01; 08,18,01; 08,20,01; NTB court transcripts 18.04.2012). However, after his conviction, Breivik has characterized himself as a Fascist.[15] Second, on several occasions he expressed support for Israel and its right to defend itself against the Jihadists (Police interview 08,06,01; NTB court transcripts 19.04.2012). Third, he tried to use Christianity for what it is worth, although it quickly turned out to be a rather vague attempt, as he is not adhering to Christianity as a personal faith, but rather due to the cultural traditions of Christianity (Police interviews 08,02; 08,03,01; NTB court transcripts 18.04.2012). Breivik's motivation for presenting these three views may be that he thought this would attract sympathizers from a broad political platform, since most people tend to dislike both National Socialism and anti-Semitism, in addition to the fact that most Norwegians and other Europeans adhere to Christian culture and traditions – at least to some extent. On the other side, one may question the realism of this ideological path, as the same people he tries to reach out to in this way, will have nothing but contempt for his ideology, which is strongly linked with racism, fascism and other violent ideologies – not to forget his actions. During the trial, he tried hard to avoid any reference to the Crusader imagery so prominent in his compendium, as he had by then realized that this rhetoric was a failure.

In his compendium Breivik concretized his enemy image by listing potential target groups and objects. This was in accordance with his stated focus on the Muslims and the Cultural-Marxists, but at the same time he stayed clear of any targets linked to Jews and the state of Israel.[16] In his compendium he clarified his target preferences through a listing of Western European primary targets and a categorization system on the individual level. The first one focused on attacks against massive and compact buildings. He mentions the MA100 political parties (*Marxist/ Multiculturalist Alliance*),[17] media conferences, individual assassinations, EU headquarters, government buildings, major multicultural buildings, media houses, certain universities, any major Muslim targets, mosques and Islamic cultural centres (Berwick 2011: 930). One strategy considered by Breivik was to attack Muslim targets in order to provoke the Muslims to enter the Jihadi arena, so that they would mobilize against the Europeans – all in order to polarize the situation and ultimately leading to a confrontation between the Muslims and the Europeans (Berwick 2011: 931). He later dismissed this idea as it would backfire.

DOI: 10.1057/9781137579973.0007

In his compendium, Breivik also constructed a categorization system for his enemies on an individual level, sorting them into the letter categories A, B, C or D, indicating their importance, and implicitly their value, as targets (Berwick 2011: 939–40). A, B and C individuals were all considered traitors, while those in category D were merely facilitating for the B and C traitors. Category A traitors were defined as political leaders, media leaders, cultural leaders and industry leaders, all qualified for death punishment. Category B traitors were the Cultural Marxists / Multi-Cultural politicians and individuals from different professional groups, such as media, teachers, writers, cartoonists, artists, celebrities and scientists. These were also qualified for death punishment. Category C traitors were seen as less influential than A and B persons, and represented targets of a lower priority. Punishment was to be fines, incarceration and expropriation. Category D individuals had little or no political influence, but were facilitating for Level B and C traitors. Here the punishment was set to none. According to this categorization, it stands out as a contradiction in terms that Breivik actually attacked the youths at Utøya at all, since he admitted that they were in fact to be considered as category C traitors (Police interview 08,03,01; NTB court transcripts 19.04.2012). His claim during the trial that many of the young victims killed had leadership positions in the youth movement was a weak attempt on post-rationalization (NTB court transcripts 19.04.2012; Berwick 2011: 950). He also argued that when he could not get the most attractive targets he would have to go further down on his list of priorities, disclosing pragmatics in practice (Police interview 08,03,01; NTB court transcripts 19.04.2012).

Moral constraints and selectiveness in targeting

If we look for moral constraints with impact on Breivik before the attacks, there were some. Despite the fact that he did not have any limits relating to the number of casualties within his set enemy categories, he claimed to have taken into consideration the so-called *civilian loss factor*, meaning that killing civilians outside his defined target groups should be avoided or kept at a minimum. In an early phase after the attacks he stated that as much as 50% civilian losses would be acceptable, and that less than 10% would be optimal (Police interviews 08,01; 08,26,01). Regarding victims, Breivik emphasized in the compendium that women

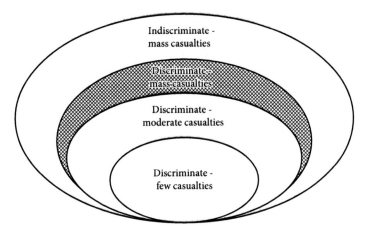

FIGURE 4.1   *Level of discrimination / casualty focus*
Source: Cato Hemmingby.

had to be killed alongside men (Berwick 2011: 942). On the other side, it seemed important for him not to be considered a child killer, which was to become significantly problematic for him after the attacks, since 33 youths killed were under age 18, whereas two were just 14 years old.[18]

If seen within a simple typology (Figure 4.1) related to the level of discrimination and number of victims, then Breivik is best placed in the category discriminate targeting with mass casualty focus. This means that he had a wide scope of target alternatives, in reality only exceeded by actors practicing totally indiscriminate attacks with mass casualty potential.

The strategy of a massive "shock-attack"

Breivik's ideology took form as he worked on his compendium, and so did his main strategy. However, what were Breivik's strategic objectives and how was he going to achieve them? The answer to the first question is found in Breivik's declared four motives for the terrorist attacks, as presented during the trial, namely (1) attention to the cause, (2) distribution of the compendium, (3) to hold responsible those accountable for promoting the multiculturalism in Norway and (4) to launch a provocation leading to persecution of the moderate cultural conservatives, in turn boosting their motivation for resistance (NTB court transcripts

DOI: 10.1057/9781137579973.0007

23.04.2012). As illustrated, Breivik's four objectives are linked and cross-linked to *advertisement, compliance, endorsement* and *provocation,* although we can obviously conclude that the three last-mentioned were unrealistic and far-fetched.[19] Rightly the terrorist received some endorsement from sympathizers after the attacks, first and foremost through letters and tributes on social media, but these were to a large degree from extremists abroad. Furthermore, the attention and the admiration on social media, seems to be decreasing from 2013. Breivik himself expressed that the attacks might be condemned today, but understood in the future, but that does not alter the fact that the ambitions were way beyond a realistic scenario (Police interviews 08,21,01; 11762579; NTB court transcripts 17.04.2012; 19.04.2012; 23.04.2012).

Through the 22 July attacks Breivik achieved two of his declared objectives, namely maximum advertisement and distribution of his compendium. Although he could just have distributed his compendium on the Internet from home without conducting the horrific attacks, he then would not get the overwhelming media coverage and attention that followed the attacks. Naturally, he boosted the fear factor in the Norwegian society, but mostly so while it was unclear whether two other cells existed or not – which did not last for long after his capture. On the other hand, it is clear that the terrorist failed with the two last declared objectives. He failed to hold the "responsible" accountable, as the Labour Party received massive support in the aftermath of the terrorist acts. Neither were there any signs of persecution of the so-called moderate cultural conservatives (NTB court transcripts 23.04.2012). In addition, Breivik failed totally to understand how counter-productive slaughtering innocent and defenceless civilians really are, and the contempt that immediately follows.

Seen in retrospect, the most crucial decision Breivik made regarding the catastrophic end-result came with his determination to launch a devastating "shock-attack". This was a strategy he devoted considerable attention to in his compendium (Berwick 2011: 950–73). It is not apparent exactly when he took this decision, but it is also a fact that he never considered anything else in concrete plans. This *one-off mass casualty approach* was also in contrast to the practice of most other solo terrorists, who have prioritized a series of small-scale attacks in some kind of war of attrition.[20] Breivik reasoned cynically that a brutal and devastating *spectacular* (operation) would boost the fear factor and ensure him global media attention. Taking his narcissistic personality disorder into

DOI: 10.1057/9781137579973.0007

consideration, this would also get him into the Hall of famous terrorists as one of the worst (or most lethal) terrorists through history. This was probably counting as an attractive compensation for the more or less failed youth politician and businessman, who during police interviews and trial tried to appear as above-average intelligent – in general regarding himself as one of the greatest terrorists ever. The latter point is clearly illustrated in Breivik's correspondence with the authors, where he commented on a remark Bjørgo made as an expert witness during the trial, saying that Breivik was an "above average competent terrorist".[21] That was seemingly not good enough for Breivik, who wrote;

> It is not correct that I merely am an "above average militant revolutionary", as I possess more competence areas than both [Muhammed] Atta and [Timothy] McVeigh. I would therefore be interested in learning which successful solo militants in any political camp, through history, you think possess more areas of competence than me ☺. You will not find anyone ☺. In any case, good luck with your project, Bjørgo and Hemmingby! ☺ A narcissistic and revolutionary salute from Anders Behring Breivik

Regarding the fear factor, Breivik was probably right, thinking that a single extremely brutal mass-casualty operation generally creates more fear than a number of small-scale attacks. However, a prerequisite for maintaining a constant fear over time is that the authorities and public believe that there are more terrorists left out there ready to strike. It is after all the expectation of more violence that gets the wanted behaviour, if it is going to work at all (Schelling 2008: 87). This explains why Breivik claimed there were two other cells ready for immediate attacks from the moment he was apprehended, in addition to his organizational claim regarding the Knight Templar network. He never admitted this to be a bluff, even if evidence weighted heavily against it. On the other hand, the threshold for carrying out such extreme actions is too high even for most solo terrorists. This is partly because of the brutality it involves, making it too difficult psychologically and emotionally to carry through, but also because it would create a high amount of contempt and condemnation against the responsible perpetrator, making the operation counter-productive. Interestingly, Breivik's grand inspiration with regard to means and methods came from the attack on the World Trade Centre in 1993 and Timothy McVeigh's bombing in Oklahoma in 1995 (Police interview nr 11762579; NTB court transcripts 20.04.2012). Accordingly, it seems as Breivik decided on the methods before the target objects. Firearms were for so-called bonus operations only.

DOI: 10.1057/9781137579973.0007

Who to attack?

Based on his perceived enemy picture, Breivik had the choice of three main directions for his targeting. He could have acted against the Muslims and Islamists as they represented the external enemy; he could choose to strike the enemy within (the traitors); or he could go for both of these groups, since complexity was not necessarily an obstacle. As for the inner enemy, the political elite and the decision-makers held *responsible* for the development of the society in general, distinguished themselves as attractive targets. Breivik was particularly obsessed with the Labour Party, who at the time was the leading party in the government coalition with the prime minister in front. However, if not settling for the elite, Breivik could also choose to strike against the so-called "Cultural Marxists" he accused of assisting and facilitating for the development. This would include different parts of the political and societal establishment, for example journalists, teachers, bureaucrats, artists, scientists and celebrities.

So why did Breivik choose to attack the Labour Party and Cultural Marxists, and not the Muslims and immigrants? According to Breivik, he initially considered striking the Muslims and immigrants like so many other far-right extremists have done before him. However, he claimed to have dismissed this option thinking years back on the racist murder of Benjamin Hermansen in January 2001 – long before Breivik himself turned to terrorism (Berwick 2011: 1394; Police interview 08,16,01). Having a mother from Norway and father from Ghana, the 15-year old boy was assaulted and killed by three neo-Nazis from the skinhead group Boot Boys in Oslo. According to Breivik, the massive public rage and condemnation following this killing proved to him that attacks against immigrants had a counter-productive effect for the right-wing movement. Hence, for him it was in no way a gesture of sympathy with the killed coloured youth, but rather a rational assessment from a strategic point of view when Breivik acknowledged that the goals for the operation was best achieved by attacking those "traitors" responsible for the situation and their accomplices (Police interview 08,16,01; NTB court transcripts 19.04.2012; 23.04.2012). Breivik's sights were therefore set on the Labour Party and the "Cultural Marxists".

Recognizing that a brutal "shock-attack" on the internal enemy was to prefer, Breivik found that doing it alone gave the best chance of success. In court he referred to how the white supremacy-group The Order had

DOI: 10.1057/9781137579973.0007

been disrupted by law enforcement agencies in the mid-1980s due to infiltration (NTB court transcripts 17.04.2012; 20.04.2012).[22] Breivik therefore never even tried to involve others as he started planning his actions. Through the whole operational phase he made a point of avoiding any overt or covert contact with domestic militant nationalists due to the risk of being detected by the security police – consciously accepting that this self-imposed restriction would reduce both operational capacity and speed. He preferred to prioritize operational security. In his compendium, as shown below, Breivik made an overview where he drew lines between the number of perpetrators, labour time required to complete the operation and risk of detection (Berwick 2011: 1472).

The following chart illustrates labour required vs. risk of apprehension for individuals who are NOT already on any watch list.

Risk vs. Labour	Time required to complete	Risk of apprehension
1 person	30 days	30%
2 people	20 days	60%
3 people	16 days	85%
4 people	13 days	90%
5 people	12 days	90–95%

Looking at this overview in the aftermath of the 22 July attacks, it is clear that Breivik miscalculated quite much on the time required for one person only, especially for a complex terrorist operation. However, it is more realistic if the ambition is reduced to simpler attack types and methods. Regarding the risk of apprehension, his calculations seem more realistic, in the sense that the risk is significantly bigger for groups than single individuals. This has been exemplified quite clearly with militant Islamist.[23]

Persistence and thoroughness compensated for weak background

Regarding capacity, little from Breivik's personal background made him a particularly resourceful and capable solo terrorist. He did not stand out as an extraordinary or specially gifted pupil in school. Neither was he particularly successful in the jobs he had after leaving school, with the legal business activity he initiated or with his political activity in

DOI: 10.1057/9781137579973.0007

the Progress party. On the other hand he was quite successful when he produced and sold fake American university diplomas from 2002 to 2006 (NTB court transcripts 19.04.2012). Regarding technical or special skills that could be of significant help for an individual planning a major terrorist operation, there were none. In fact, Breivik had not even done compulsory military service, similar to most Norwegian young males at his age did. Naturally the terrorist later regretted missing this opportunity to acquire military skills (Police interview 08,25; NTB court transcripts 17.04.2012). As a result of this, Breivik had very limited shooting experience before the 22 July attacks. He tried the rifle a few times and he was for a period of some months active in a sports pistol club, but that was really it. Almost needless to say, there was no previous knowledge whatsoever with regard to the use of explosives (Police interview 08,03,01; NTB court transcripts 19.04.2012). As illustrated, Breivik did not have a very suitable background for a man with ambitions to conduct a massive, complex two-folded terrorist operation. However, Breivik did compensate for his, in this specific context, weak background in several ways.

First of all, Breivik's ability to stay focused and motivated over a very long period was essential. Despite the fact that it is somewhat unclear exactly when he did decide to commit a terrorist operation, it was nevertheless a project that went on for several years. This demands a high degree of long-lasting motivation, persistence and focus from the perpetrator's side. Second, Breivik obviously had an adequate ability to plan and operationalize a complex operation and not everyone would be able to do that. Third, his extreme and somewhat exaggerated, and by some ridiculed, security consciousness, enabled him to avoid detection during the long phases of planning, preparation and execution of the attacks. Rightly, a few persons in his close surroundings did note his radical and extremist statements from time to time, but he never disclosed that he was planning violent actions (NOU 2012: 14, 355). Finally, Breivik was to demonstrate thoroughness in the bomb-production. Rightly, the bomb itself was not of the same quality as for example the Provisional IRA achieved on a regular basis relating to effect, but it nevertheless killed several people and caused substantial material damage as it went off.[24] Furthermore, he did not choose the easiest path as he constructed his fertilizer-bomb, and he persistently overcame problems he encountered in the process. However, it should be noted as a contradiction to this thoroughness, that Breivik's understanding of how explosives actually work when detonating was very limited. During police interviews he made some sketches, illustrating pre-attack thoughts he had with regard to the positioning of the bomb vehicle outside the H-building in the Government District, in order to make the building collapse (Police interview 08,08,01). The way he thought he could direct and control the blast did indeed illustrate that this part was more based on far-fetched assumptions, rather than knowledge. Hence, it all comes down to the fact that he was mostly competent at building the bomb, but the result was nevertheless to be disastrous.

Funding is always a critical part of complex or continuous terrorist activity, and Breivik did have a good starting point. The police investigation revealed that the terrorist had earned 3,687,588 NOK (approximately 420,000 GBP or 682,000 USD[25]) on selling false university documents in the period from 2002 to 2006. Using foreign bank accounts he avoided taxes on most of this income.[26] A part of the profits was later invested in the stock market, but without any significant success. When the terrorist in 2006 moved to his mother's flat, Breivik claimed that he had approximately 500,000–600,000 NOK (56,800–68, 000 GBP) in the bank and approximately 300,000 NOK (approximately 34,000 GBP) in cash. Furthermore, in autumn 2009 he applied for and got ten credit cards. This provided him with an extra money reserve of 235,000 NOK (26,700 GBP) in extra funding.[27] As illustrated, with limited living expenses from 2006, the terrorist had quite a satisfactory financial situation. Just as importantly, without a regular job he had time to devote himself totally to the operation. This partially compensated for the fact that he, as a solo terrorist, had to do everything himself, in contradiction to a group that can assign different tasks on the members. A last point worth noting regarding Breivik's operational capacity is that he did not seek to escape. Offenders, who intend to keep going until physically confronted by law enforcement personnel, will under normal circumstances be able to operate over a longer period, compared with offenders seeking to escape, hence also expanding their lethal potential.

A terrorist versus a peaceful society

It is important to remember the external factors and the societal context the terrorist operated within. Until the 22 July attacks, the Norwegian society had been blessed with an absence of major terrorist incidents. There had been a handful of violent right-wing attacks, but these were

DOI: 10.1057/9781137579973.0007

not grave enough to put societal security on top of the political agenda of any Norwegian government. Nor did this subject concern the voters. As Cathrine Sandnes brilliantly wrote in the newspaper Dagbladet;[28]

> *Barely any of us were capable of envisioning a terrorist act of this kind in Norway, and just a few were interested in new (counterterrorism) efforts and restrictions. And the fewest of us have wished for politicians prioritizing counterterrorism preparedness rather than school, health or better roads.*

The planned closure of the Grubbegata street in the Government District was to serve as the ultimate illustration of bureaucratic and political negligence regarding security efforts before 22 July 2011. In 2003, the Prime Minister's Office tasked the Directorate of Police to do a threat assessment with regard to the security for government members and the physical objects concerned (NOU 2012: 14, 423). In June 2004, the report was discussed in the government's security cabinet. Two months later the government decided to follow up on the report, which recommended no less than 179 concrete steps to enhance the security – including closure of the Grubbegata street (NOU 2012: 14, 427). The Ministry of Administration, Reform and Church affairs (FAD) was assigned to handle this, but the street closure turned out to become a particular nut to crack.

In 2006, project leader Christian Fredrik Horst in FAD, made it clear on national television that the main vulnerability at the time was a car or truck loaded with explosives, driving unhindered right into the centre of the Government District. However, this did not spark any rapid response on bureaucratic or political top level.[29] It must be added though, that the government's indecisiveness in the matter, was accompanied by the same degree of indecisiveness from the Oslo municipality's conservative-led political leadership, and also protests from commercial interests, neighbours and news media. In 2007 an editorial titled "*Hypothetical and hysterical*", in the major Norwegian newspaper Aftenposten, slammed and ridiculed the proposed street closure.[30] The case dragged out in time and in hindsight, the Grubbegata-affair had all the symptoms of a ludicrous travesty, and one man exploited this nonconformity gravely.

Personnel from the Norwegian Government Security and Service Organization (GSSO) were in July 2011 (and still are) securing the Government District.[31] The security personnel were unarmed and the physical security measures were limited – in reality only scaled for minor security threats. Seemingly, much was based on the assumption that the

DOI: 10.1057/9781137579973.0007

Norwegian Police Security Service (PST) would be able to detect any terrorist threat through the intelligence-driven approach. PST itself was affected by the historical developments. A few small-scale incidents with far-right extremists the last decades had by now been overshadowed by the growing threat from militant Islamists. Also, the Ministry of Justice and Police had stated that international terrorism should be a priority for the service (NOU 2012: 14, 363, 366). In addition, limited resources forced PST to focus on on-going cases, at the expense of other preventive functions (NOU 2012: 14, 367).

Overall, the peaceful Norwegian society was in 2011 vulnerable for serious terrorist attacks, and Anders Behring Breivik's profile was not a part of the dominating threat picture.

Notes

1   Breivik's troubled childhood and the failed attempt to have him sent to a foster home are described in detail in Borchgrevink (2013). *A Norwegian Tragedy: Anders Behring Breivik and the* Massacre at Utøya. Cambridge: Polity; and Seierstad (2015). *One of Us*. London: Virago.

2   Oslo District Court – Judgment 2012-08-24 TOSLO-2011-188627-24E

3   Oslo District Court – Judgment 2012-08-24 TOSLO-2011-188627-24E

4   Langset, Kristin Grue (2011). *Breivik har vært medlem og har hatt verv i ungdomspartiet*. Aftenposten.

5   Oslo District Court – Judgment 2012-08-24 TOSLO-2011-188627-24E

6   Oslo District Court – Judgment 2012-08-24 TOSLO-2011-188627-24E

7   Breivik's failed political career is described in Seierstad (2015).

8   Oslo District Court – Judgment 2012-08-24 TOSLO-2011-188627-24E

9   Oslo District Court – Judgment 2012-08-24 TOSLO-2011-188627-24E

10   VG Nett (2012). *Foreløpig psykiatrisk vurdering av forhold rundt Anders Behring Breivik*. A report by Randi Rosenqvist.

11   Other solo terrorists with personalized ideologies are, for example, Theodore Katcinzky and Franz Funchs.

12   A good example of the ZOG worldview is shown by the white supremacy-leader and author William Pierce (aka Andrew Macdonald) in his novels *The Turner Diaries* (1980) and *The Hunter* (1989). For a further discussion of the conspiratorial worldviews and enemy images, see Tore Bjørgo (1995), Extreme Nationalism and Violent Discourser in Scandinavia: "The Resistance", "Traitors", and "Foreign Invaders", in Bjørgo, T. (ed.) *Terror from the Extreme Right*. London: Frank Cass.

DOI: 10.1057/9781137579973.0007

13   This phenomenon is extensively covered in Moghaddam, Fathali M. (2008). *How Globalization Spurs Terrorism*. Westport: Praeger.

14   As described in general by Crenshaw, Martha (2011). *Explaining Terrorism*. Oxon: Routledge, 49.

15   Breivik's self-identification as a fascist was probably influenced by several expert witnesses on political ideologies, who during the trial characterized Breivik's ideology as a variety of fascism, based on his compendium and statements in court. Breivik apparently accepted this label and later claimed from his prison cell that he intended to establish the Norwegian Fascist Party.

16   However, some of Breivik's writings from prison after his conviction became more anti-Semitic in character.

17   MA100 is an abbreviation of the cultural Marxist/Multiculturalist Alliance 100 and describes the current West European political establishment of political parties who indirectly or directly supports the "islamization" of Europe. Berwick: 933

18   Oslo District Court – Judgment 2012-08-24 TOSLO-2011-188627-24E

19   See Martha Crenshaw Hutchinson, *Revolutionary Terrorism*, 41–85; T.P. Thornton (1965), Terror as a Weapon of Political Agitation, in H. Eckstein (ed.) *Internal War*. New York: The Free Press of Glencoe.

20   For example Theodore Kaztinsky, John Ausonius, Franz Fuchs, David Copeland and Peter Mangs.

21   In written correspondence from Breivik to the authors, dated 02.11.2012.

22   The Order was operating in the United States in the 1980s. It was founded by Robert Jay Mathews, who was killed in a confrontation with police in 1984.

23   See more on this subject in Chapter 8 on comparative perspectives.

24   Assessments regarding bomb quality and effect are based on information retrieved by Cato Hemmingby from various sources with EOD expertise.

25   The estimates in GBP and USD are based on the exchange rate on 22 July 2011.

26   Oslo District Court – Judgment 2012-08-24 TOSLO-2011-188627-24E

27   Oslo District Court – Judgment 2012-08-24 TOSLO-2011-188627-24E

28   Sandnes, Cathrine (2012). «*Blir vi et bedre samfunn av å sparke folk til de ikke reiser seg igjen?*». Feature article in Dagbladet.

29   NRK Østlandssendingen (2006). *Advarte om bomben i 2006.*

30   Aftenposten Aften (2007). *Hypotetisk og hysterisk.* Editorial, 26.02.2007. In 2012 the leader of the Conservative party running the Oslo municipality actually admitted that Aftenposten's editorial was something he took into account; Bergens Tidende (2012). *Røsland: Grubbegata kunne ha vært stengt før.*

31   GSSO is an institution under the Norwegian Ministry of Local Government and Modernisation (KMD).

DOI: 10.1057/9781137579973.0007

5
From Thinking to Acting

Abstract: *Breivik's operational phase had a long timeline and was complex of nature. It became a highly dynamic process, with a substantial amount of unpredictability involved. Most importantly this chapter illustrates how even the most ruthless terrorist acted under a number of constraints. Furthermore, uncontrollable factors such as coincidences, luck and bad luck did have an effect on the operation and the targeting process.*

Keywords: bomb construction; compendium; constraints; farm; funding; hostile reconnaissance; manifesto; plans; preparations

Hemmingby, Cato, and Tore Bjørgo. *The Dynamics of a Terrorist Targeting Process: Anders B. Breivik and the 22 July Attacks in Norway.* Basingstoke: Palgrave Macmillan, 2016. DOI: 10.1057/9781137579973.0008.

As Breivik sat in his mother's flat, developing his compendium, ideology and strategy, concrete ideas and plans started to take shape. However, as he moved towards the realization of these he was soon to experience the complexity of interaction relating to the target selection process. In fact, different practical problems and constraints were to haunt him until the very day of the attacks, and in court he claimed that he probably had changed his plans approximately 20–30 times, often to his frustration (NTB court transcripts 20.04.2012). To identify and time-set the concrete plans Breivik made is challenging, and the potential pitfalls are many. One factor contributing to this is the huge amount of speculations and inaccurate suggestions in the media, but Breivik's numerous statements in police interviews and from the trial also makes it difficult to grasp. He talked so willingly and much about everything on different occasions, that it is sometimes difficult to clarify what was really considered and planned before the 22 July attacks, and what have been merely loose ideas or thoughts of the moment in the aftermath, trying to rationalize his actions. Some of his statements have also been rather unstructured at times, leaving room for doubts, speculations and misinterpretations. Furthermore, his personality disorder and narcissistic personality opens for the possibility that he during police interviews and the trial tried to present his plans and ideas as more thoroughly considered than they in reality have been. There are several indications of this, but that said, some stated ideas and plans are more consistent and trust-worthy than others.

What seems to have been the first concrete, main plan in the planning process, which he according to himself devoted a lot of time on, involved three vehicle-born IEDs (Improvised Explosive Devices) against different targets, followed by three shooting attacks against different objects (Police interview 08,03,01; NTB court transcripts 19.04.2012). With reference to the target overview Level 2 objects, the perpetrator had a range of possible targets to consider – a process that was to become partly simple and partly complicated. The simple part was that the H-building in the Government District, housing the Prime Minister's Office from floors 13 to 17 and the Ministry of Justice and Police from floors 2 to 12, always was the undisputable target number one. This iconic building, housing the Labour Party-lead coalition government and bureaucrats that Breivik held accountable for the Cultural Marxist take-over of Norwegian society, was the perfect target. The fact that other ministries surrounded the H-building was considered a bonus, boosting the attack with regard to the *accountable*-perspective. The Labour Party's HQ building on Youngstorget square, located almost next to the Government District, was a seemingly clear target number two. However, Breivik claims to have made some reflections regarding the civilian loss-factor, much due to other buildings in the area. He specifically mentioned the offices belonging to the Norwegian Tourist Association, located on the side of the same building-complex, and he reckoned many would be killed if the HQ-building collapsed as a result of the bombing. Nonetheless, Breivik confirmed in court that the Labour Party-building remained to be target number two on the list even after the civilian loss-considerations. Like the H-building in the Government District, the Labour Party HQ building is a well-known and historic building, and as such an iconic target object, even though it is not visually standing out in the urban surroundings as much as the tall government building.

Interestingly, Breivik had substantial difficulties in deciding on bomb target number three, almost to the degree that he did not quite know what to use the third IED for. He considered several buildings in Oslo, more specifically the Parliament building, the Parliament district (or block) nearby, the Oslo City Hall, the newspaper Aftenposten's building, the Directorate of Immigration and the Royal Palace (Police interview 08,15 01). However, some of these lacked attractive features and some had to be dismissed for other reasons. The Directorate of Immigration was probably not an adequate high-symbolic object, and it was also located rather anonymously in a tight and busy neighbourhood. Here the potential for an (for Breivik) unacceptable civilian loss potential was also a consideration. The civilian loss factor also put the newspaper Aftenposten out of the question with regard to a big bomb. This because the newspaper, located close to the Oslo central train station, only occupied a small part of the building. If the construction had given in as a result of a bomb blast, then most victims would be other people than Aftenposten employees. The Oslo City Hall was also a difficult target for a bomb attack. First of all it was housing the conservative-lead Oslo municipality administration, including local politicians from the Progress party Breivik had been an active member in. Second, the iconic building's central location in downtown Oslo, normally crowded with tourists as well as locals, made it an unpredictable target regarding civilian losses (Police interview 08,29,01). The potential civilian casualty perspective was also a point he considered with regard to the iconic Parliament building, and furthermore the terrorist was unsure

DOI: 10.1057/9781137579973.0008

how to get the vehicle in a good position. As for the Parliament district, this is an ordinary block consisting of office buildings belonging to the Parliament, and it stands out as a rather unattractive alternative with regard to symbolism, and the perpetrator would also here have little control over potential casualties in a massive bomb blast. On the other side, the Royal Palace definitely had attractive features since it is a highly iconic building overlooking the Karl Johan Street, and in a satisfactory distance from other buildings or crowded areas. Breivik also stated that it was a factor that a blown-up palace would be observed from the normally crowded and long high street of Oslo, the Karl Johan Street, something that would not be the case (at least not just as much) with the iconic Parliament building (Police interview 08,29,01). In addition, the mid-entrance for arriving cars under the palace would make it easy to get the bomb vehicle directly under the building. Breivik therefore ended up with the Royal Palace as the third bomb target, but with an unusual and almost ironic prerequisite: the royal family could not be present at the time of the detonation, due to the fact that he considered himself to be a monarchist (Police interviews 08,02; 08,03,01). The strong position the royal family have in the Norwegian society may have played a part in the considerations. Accordingly, bomb number three should first and foremost be a warning to the royal family with regard to their immigrant-friendly attitude (Police interview 11762579, 08.02.2012).

After placing the last bomb vehicle at the palace his plan was to rush to the Blitz anarchist house nearby and shoot as many as possible, before moving on to the newspaper Dagsavisen a few blocks away and finally the Socialist Left Party's HQ. All of these objects are located relatively close to each other, as well as to the chosen bomb targets, so the geographical location of the potential targets did probably have influence on this part of the initial plan. Another indication of this is that Breivik also considered including the Norwegian Broadcasting Corporation (NRK) for a shooting attack. This would without a doubt be a far more prestigious target, compared with the three shooting attack objects previously mentioned. NRK is the national broadcaster in Norway and attacking it would be fully in accordance with his declared hatred and focus against the news media in general. Here it can be mentioned that the former party leader of the Progress Party (that Breivik once was a member of) Carl I. Hagen, for a period of time consequently called the broadcasting corporation for the Labour Party Broadcasting Corporation, using the acronym ARK instead of NRK. He claimed that NRK treated the Progress Party unfavourably, for example in debates during election campaigns.[1] Breivik did actually go to the broadcaster's facilities at Marienlyst in Oslo in order to consider the possibilities, but it seems that he quickly dismissed it as a potential target. One reason was the geographical location, but just as important, Breivik lacked knowledge of how it was inside the buildings. He expected there would be security zones inside the buildings, after the principle of compartmentalization, and he felt insecure how this would affect a shooting attack (Police interview 08,29,01). This is why he, after the three car-bombs, settled for the Blitz anarchist house, the newspaper Dagsavisen and the Socialist Left Party's HQ as shooting targets. Furthermore, he would simply keep going until the police stopped him. However, it must be noted that all the time the most important part was the bombs; the shooting attacks were secondary (NTB court transcripts 20.04.2012).

Adjusting to three bombs and one shooting target

At one point early in the planning process Breivik modified the idea with three bombs and three shooting attacks. He decided to change to a plan for three bombs, combined with only one small arms-attack at a fourth location (NTB court transcripts 19.04.2012). The time and reason for this decision remain somewhat unclear, but at least three factors may have influenced his change of plan. First, the anarchist Blitz house would only be crowded and attractive on Friday or Saturday nights, and this corresponded badly with the timing at the other target objects, since they had to be attacked on daytime – possibly with the exception of the Royal Palace (Police interview 08,29,01). Second, compared with public events gathering lots of people, the mass-casualty potential was more unpredictable on the three potential shooting objects. Third, he might have feared that he could be confronted and stopped by police before he reached all the shooting targets, since he then would be operating downtown all the time, quite close to the bombing targets that would attract a lot of law enforcement capacities. As the bombing targets remained to be the same, he therefore now set his sights on the SKUP annual prize conference for investigative journalism for the single shooting attack. This was to be arranged 1–3 April 2011, at Quality Hotel in Tønsberg, about 100 km from Oslo. If he was unable to be ready in time for the SKUP conference, his target alternative was to be the annual Labour

Party convention 7–10 April one week later (Police interview 08,29,01; NTB court transcripts19.04.2012). The short time-difference between the SKUP-conference and the back-up event indicates that the self-confident terrorist only expected minor delays. Also worth noting, the back-up target was in accordance with his compendium, where he specifically mentioned that the annual meetings of the socialist or social democrat parties in Europe as prioritized targets (Berwick 2011: 951).

According to Breivik, he also thought loosely about what to do if he failed to produce the necessary amount of explosives for large bombs. In that case he thought about how to use small bombs, or a combination of a large bomb with one or two small bombs of approximately 50 kg, against news media targets. For example, he claims to have thought about delivering a small bomb to the newspaper Aftenposten wearing a FedEx uniform. He also claims to have considered the broadcasting company NRK and the VG newspaper for such alternative attacks, although both locations were inconvenient. However, it must be underlined that there are no indications that Breivik did seriously plan or make practical preparations for any such alternative small plans, and it should be regarded as very superficial thoughts only. On the other hand Breivik stated that with just one big bomb, he had to choose one target for that and one for the shooting attack, which was to be the media conference SKUP (NTB court transcripts 19.04.2012).

The first documented signs of practical preparations from Breivik's part are from 2009. On 18 May 2009, Breivik registered the agricultural company Breivik Geofarm (which the terrorist renamed to A Geofarm in March 2011). For Breivik this was a necessity to establish a plausible cover, as he wanted to rent a farm for the bomb production, and not least to be able to buy fertilizer and other components necessary.[2] A few months later, in September–October 2009, he also acquired ten credit cards from different financial institutions, which ensured him 235,000 NOK (at the time equal to 26,700 GBP or 43,500 USD) in extra funding.[3] At this time he also had determined a strategy for the best possible distribution of his compendium, namely to e-mail it to as many people as possible, and preferably to potential sympathizers. From November 2009 to February 2010 he therefore systematically collected e-mail addresses through two Facebook-accounts (Police interview 08,07).

From 2010 Breivik started to make the necessary investments, including acquiring weapons. The Benelli shotgun, which was left unused during the terrorist attacks, had been legally bought in 2003, after Breivik had

DOI: 10.1057/9781137579973.0008

completed a hunting qualification course. Regarding other weapons, the terrorist initially conducted an unsuccessful search on the black market, even abroad in the Czech Republic. More specifically, he travelled to Prague in the late summer of 2010 with two objectives in mind. He wanted to get accurate Norwegian police insignia replicas from a local print shop, since he was afraid of detection if he did this in Norway. More vaguely documented, Breivik also claims he was looking for weapons (NTB court transcripts, 19.04.2012). He got his insignias, but finding weapons proved difficult and he found it easier to acquire weapons legally. He bought the Mini-Ruger rifle in November 2010 and the Glock pistol in March 2011 – both legally (Police interview 08,07; NOU 2012: 14, 348-34). The rifle was in a category included in the hunting regulations and getting the licence for this weapon was more or less a formality, taking into consideration that he had the qualifying course. As for the pistol, Breivik enrolled in a pistol sports shooting club in Oslo. By being an active member for half a year or more, the terrorist got the documentation needed. The club confirmed his active membership to the police authorities handling weapons applications, and Breivik bought his Glock pistol in a store in Oslo. In general, Breivik purchased most of the equipment he needed for the operation between May and July 2010, although he undertook purchases as late as June 2011.[4] Breivik acted cautiously as he bought weapon accessories, protection gear or items linked to the bomb production. However, on a few occasions he was forced to accept some risk, primarily as he bought sodium nitrate from a pharmacy, when he ordered the 15 meter powder fuse from Poland and when he ordered 150 kg aluminium powder from Poland (NOU 2012: 14, 353).

In December 2010, as part of an international cooperation effort, Norwegian customs authorities passed on a list to the Norwegian Police Security Service (PST), disclosing money transactions between Norwegian customers and a listed Polish company. The overview did not show what kind of goods that had been bought, but merely the names of the customers and the amount of money involved. The list with 41 names included Breivik who had paid approximately $20 for a 15 meters long fuse, but as the product type did not show, and it was in fact the smallest sum of money on the list, no actions were taken. Although the list from the customs did not get appropriate follow-up by the police security service, the 22 July commission did not find sufficient reason to claim that PST should have detected Breivik in advance (NOU 2012: 14, 380, 393, 395).

DOI: 10.1057/9781137579973.0008

Information gathering and reconnaissance

Breivik claims to have based his information gathering on three main sources, namely the media, different Internet sites and physical hostile reconnaissance. From ordinary news media, both paper and online sources, Breivik followed what was going on in general. He could also to a certain degree register the activities of central politicians. Not least, the terrorist could keep himself up to date on the planned closure of the Grubbegata street in the Government District (Police interview 08,26,01).

Using a variety of Internet resources Breivik also looked up information about the specific locations of institutions, details on the areas surrounding these, and also more specific details regarding the buildings. He also tried to look into the activities of different ministers, as well as events coordinated by the ministries (Police interview 08,26,01). This was not necessarily such a clandestine activity as it might sound like, due to the simple fact that much information are made public by the Prime Minister's Office and the other ministries themselves. One example is the publishing of the ministers' official weekly programs. In fact, Breivik claims he was in general very careful using his computer for more detailed information gathering, due to the fear of being "flagged" by the police security service. This was in accordance with his partially exaggerated ideas of the capacities of the police security service, which affected him in several ways. One of the best examples in this regard is that Breivik was very restrictive regarding the use of Google Street View for planning and reconnaissance. He believed that if he used this tool to look at high-value targets he could be more or less automatically detected. Another example is that he could not go on the Internet site of the Norwegian government every day, because that could be regarded as suspicious (Police interview 08,26,01). Other decisions he made relating to operational security, which made more sense, was that he consciously moderated his extreme political and ideological views when he visited far-right Internet sites and forums. This downplay from Breivik's side made it more likely that political opponents, and the security service if it ever could have been an issue, would focus on other and seemingly more extremist individuals. Finally, the perpetrator took active steps to hide his IP-addresses, which also was a rational precaution (NOU 2012: 14, 355).

Breivik was equally afraid of detection when he conducted hostile reconnaissance on site, and also here his behaviour was partially affected by a mix of clear exaggerations and more sensible considerations. For example, when he was out looking at the Government District, he believed that even a short glance at CCTV cameras would "flag" him (Police interview 08,26,01; NTB court transcripts 19.04.2012). This one exaggeration became a constraint for him, and it reduced the quality of his information gathering significantly. Overall, potential target objects he looked at on site were few, and most of them were given a quick and superficial glance. Not surprisingly, the H-building in the Government District caught most of his attention, and he claims to have conducted hostile reconnaissance there on eight occasions – four times on close range and four times observing from a distance. The four times he passed through the Government District he emphasized on blending in, for example by carrying shopping bags from stores nearby the site. On one occasion he also walked through with a friend, who was unaware of the devious intentions of the terrorist. The four reconnaissance visits he conducted from a distance, was probably of little value.

During the police investigative interviews Breivik clearly wanted to give the impression that he had conducted the reconnaissance in a professional manner, and that he had been able to gather a lot of detailed construction information – especially from the Government District's H-building that he bombed. However, the police investigative interviews found that Breivik was really not registering very much at all as he conducted physical reconnaissance. For example, when he gave the impression that he had studied the pillars of the building thoroughly as he passed by, this was easily contradicted when the interviewers started to pursue details. Another indicator supporting the theory of a poor information gathering result is that Breivik could not give up the position of a single CCTV camera, which he was seemingly very concerned with. There were approximately 200 of these in the area at that time, both outdoors and inside cameras counted, and many were easy to spot for anyone walking around in the Government District. Furthermore, his general knowledge about the capacities and facilities of the local security unit from the Government Security and Service Organization (GSSO) was so to speak non-existent. He knew nothing about their organization, manpower, operational capacities or the location of key functions, as the operations room. Nor did the terrorist register relevant security details in front of the H-building. He did for example believe that the thin plastic chain along the pavement in front, blocking most of the arrival space, was of steel. This was in fact a planned security detail, because it made it

DOI: 10.1057/9781137579973.0008

possible for the cars of the prime minister and close protection officers to drive straight through it, in case a security threat occurred at the point of arrival or departure.

One interesting aspect regarding critical national asset protection is that visible security efforts may influence the approach of a terrorist or terrorist group quite significantly, and this can be exemplified with one of Breivik's reconnaissance observations in the Government District. Among the terrorist operations inspiring him the most was the 1993 World Trade Centre bombing in New York and at a certain stage he was thinking that it would be preferably to get a bomb vehicle under the H-building. On one of his trips to the Government District he found out where the goods delivery facility leading under the ministerial complex was. However, he noticed the control established there and was unsure whether the truck was too big to get in. He therefore dropped his ideas of getting the bomb vehicle under the bomb target, without further investigations (Police interview 08,26,01, NTB court transcripts 19.04.2012). This concrete example illustrates that it is not necessarily the quality of a security measure that decides whether terrorists are deterred from approaching, but rather the pure existence of it.

As illustrated, Breivik's reconnaissance efforts were in reality of poor quality. This stands in contradiction to the statement in his own compendium, where reconnaissance was one of nine basic criteria, for conducting a successful operation (Berwick 2011: 839). On the other hand, Breivik did have a point when he stated that small details not necessarily were so important, as long as he had access and was able to drive the vehicle in front of the building (Police interview 08,26,01). For terrorists planning on using vehicle-delivered bombs, access is the one major subject of interest and importance.

Another practical constraint for the terrorist worth noticing was his class B driver's license. This limited him to vehicles with a maximum load weight of 1200 kg and he was not prepared to challenge that. First, he was afraid of being stopped by police in a routine traffic control during transport phases. Second, he was afraid of experiencing a physical breakdown of the vehicle due to load overweight. This did not have any effect on the target selection, but it established a limitation regarding the size of his planned bombs (NTB court transcripts 20.04.2012).

Relating to the psychological dimension, Breivik claims to have used meditation techniques to dis-emotionalize himself (NTB court transcripts 19.04.2012). This in order to enable him to keep personal fear

DOI: 10.1057/9781137579973.0008

and empathy at a distance, and making him able conduct the atrocities (NTB court transcripts 19.04.2012; 20.04.2012). Furthermore, it helped him keep the motivation and focus over a long period, he claimed. In the compendium, he also spent considerable space on developing an argument to "embrace and familiarise yourself with the concept of killing women, even very attractive women" (Berwick 2011, 942). It is not clear what direct effect these exercises had, but the fact is that he on the day of the attacks demonstrated a terrifying ability to kill a large number of individuals on a very short distance without any mercy.

Looking for a farm caused a serious delay

During autumn 2010 Breivik started to look for a smallholding or farm. It had to be within reasonable distance to Oslo and of an appropriate size, because this was important for the estimated amount of fertilizer he needed (Police interview 08,07; NTB court transcripts 16.04.2012). Breivik experienced significant problems finding such a place and he was seriously delayed. As time went by he widened the geographical search area considerably and he approached several lessors at the same time. On 29 March 2011 a lessor in Sunnmøre (more than 500 km from Oslo) initiated an e-mail dialogue with Breivik after the latter's Internet advertisement on an agricultural site. However, Breivik ended the correspondence days later when he was told it was an eco farm, obviously realizing that cow manure is useless for making bombs.[5] But there was another explanation to this as well, because in the meantime he found and got hold of another. On 6 April 2011 he signed a contract for the farm called Vålstua at Åsta (approximately 150 kilometres north-east of Oslo) from 1 May, and four days later he moved in.

The delay caused by the search for a farm had ruined Breivik's overall timing. Both his primary shooting attack target, the SKUP investigative journalist conference and his reserve shooting attack target, the Labour Party's annual convention some days later, had been held in April – while Breivik was busy with his search and paper work. As such, he experienced the drawback of including time-fixed events into a plan, namely the fact that time may easily become your enemy – or at least a significant constraint.

Settled at the farm in the beginning of May, Breivik was still aiming for three bombs and a shooting target object, but now he was in need of

DOI: 10.1057/9781137579973.0008

a new shooting attack target and it was at this point the Workers' Youth League camp at Utøya surfaced as alternative number one. It does not seem to have been a very complicated decision to make, because Breivik simply regarded this event as the single most attractive target for a shooting spree at this particular time of the year (NTB court transcripts 20.04.2012). That said, the camp at Utøya did not surface totally by random, since the terrorist had been keeping the event at Utøya, 38km northwest of Oslo, in mind for about a year as an alternative target (NTB court transcripts 23.04.2012). An indication that this claim has credibility can be related to the fact that a young male person unsuccessfully requested the member list of the Workers Youth League from the Ministry of Government Administration, Reform and Church Affairs (FAD) in May or June 2010 – a list the ministry did not have anyway.[6] Breivik has denied that he did this, but the person from the ministry who met the man face to face, is quite sure it was the terrorist.

Breivik disclosed a substantial degree of pragmatism in his targeting, well illustrated with the fact that the victims at Utøya were mainly what he had defined as category C traitors. According to Breivik's own compendium they were not eligible for death punishment. When pushed on this in court, Breivik said that the guidelines in the manifesto were to be followed as far as possible, but that adjustments could be made if it was not possible to reach the primary target categories (Police interview 08,03,01; NTB court transcripts 19.04.2012). Not so surprisingly, Breivik tried to rationalize his targeting by claiming that most of the youths were political leaders, which was a far-fetched attempt since the teens held different administrative, functional and ordinary membership positions in local youth groups. Also, trying to avoid the label child-killer became difficult. He (wrongly) argued that children in a legal perspective are those less than age 14, and said he assumed everybody had to be at least age 16 in order to participate at Utøya. This also underlines his rather negligent information gathering as he planned the attacks, and this also corresponds with the quality of his physical reconnaissance efforts, which were of low quality. Another peculiar aspect of the Utøya-attack was that Breivik before the operation thought that only 50% of militant nationalists would support that specific attack, but still he did it, arguing that people would understand this in the future as the situation between "Europeans" and Muslims in Europe deteriorates (NTB court transcripts 19.04.2012). This indicate an unusual degree of pragmatism on his part – or alternatively, an unusual high degree of fanaticism.

Breivik regarded Utøya as a perfect target from a tactical point of view, with up to 700 participants on a limited area, surrounded by cold water and 550 meters to the closest shore (Police interview 08,09,01). In court, Breivik was crystal clear on his intentions on Utøya, stating that "*my goal was to kill 600 people*" – first and foremost by shooting and chasing the panicking youngsters out in the cold water and making them drown, using the water as "a weapon of mass destruction" (NTB court transcripts 20.04.2012). He also hoped to catch and decapitate a top category "Cultural Marxist" visiting and talking to the youths. Breivik wanted to film the whole decapitation sequence and launch it on Internet.[7] Which person this would be was depending on the exact day of the attack, as journalist Marte Michelet was scheduled for Wednesday, Foreign Minister Jonas Gahr Støre for Thursday and former Prime Minister Gro Harlem Brundtland for Friday. Prime Minister Stoltenberg was due for a visit on Saturday, but this would not correspond with the bomb in the Government District. He was therefore in the clear, unless he would be in office at the time of the bombing.

The final plan

Breivik estimated three to four weeks to make the three bombs needed for his major plan, but it turned out to take three times as long just to make one (NTB court transcripts 19.04.2012; Police interview 08,14,01). Breivik confirmed in court that the manufacturers' efforts to make fertilizers with high nitrogen content less suitable for bomb making, made it more difficult and time-consuming to make the bombs (Police interview 08,15,01; NTB court transcripts 19.04.2012). The fact that he was running out of money also became a constraint, adding to the increasing pressure. His bank accounts were in fact empty before he moved in at the farm, from April 26, and he had to start using his pre-collected credit cards (NTB court transcripts 16.04.2012). A primary concern for Breivik was that he would not be able to pay his credit card bills when they started coming in, leading to insolvency registration in central registers. This would most likely cause him trouble when he went to lease vehicles necessary for the operation – especially the bomb vehicle he was to lease just before initiating the attacks. He was also aware that the street leading to the H-building was to be permanently closed for security reasons after years of bureaucratic and political delays (Police interview 08,26,01;

DOI: 10.1057/9781137579973.0008

NTB court transcripts 20.04.2012). Late 2010 he had in fact been worried that a Jihadi cell arrested in Oslo and Germany would speed up the street closure (Police interview 08,26,01).

As Breivik worked on the explosives with slow progress he must have realized that the timing of his planned attack on the Government District got worse every week, due to the fact that the offices are quite empty in the holiday season, from mid-June to mid-August. The politicians are not much present at all in this period, and only a limited number of bureaucrats keep the wheels in motion. He was also stressed by the planned closure of the Grubbegata street leading to his target object, as the work was in progress and due to take place in the autumn – although this was unannounced at the time. By the end of June, Breivik realized he had to carry out the attack with just one bomb, and from then on the focus was solely on a bomb action against the H-building in the Government District and the shooting attack at Utøya (Police interview 08,03,01; NTB court transcripts 19.04.2012). This plan was finally locked somewhere between June 30 and July 10 (Police interview 08,08,01). While Breivik had rented his Fiat Doblo early in April, he picked up a VW Crafter cargo van from the company AVIS in Oslo in July 15. That was the vehicle he was to load with the fertilizer-bomb and the operation was now only one week away.

Notes

1   Ringheim, Gunnar (2009). – *NRK-Takvam er mye hardere mot Siv enn Kristin.* Dagbladet.
2   Information collected from the national register; Brønnøysund Register Centre. Retrieved 9 September 2011, from www.brreg.no.
3   Oslo District Court – Judgment 2012-08-24 TOSLO-2011-188627-24E.
4   Oslo District Court – Judgment 2012-08-24 TOSLO-2011-188627-24E.
5   Nordal S. & Halkjelsvik, S. (2011). *Vurderte å leige jord til Behring Breivik.*
6   Bjordal, Nina (2012). *Breivik ringte og ba om medlemslister.* Nettavisen; Interview with the employee in question in the Norwegian Ministry for Administration, Reform and Church affairs (FAD), August 2012.
7   Police interview 08,09,01; NTB court transcripts 19.04.2012; 23.04.2012. Breivik was clearly inspired by Al-Qaida decapitations movies on this point, and he did not deny it.

6
The Attacks and the Consequences

Abstract: *A detailed reconstruction of the attacks in the government district and at Utøya illustrates the dynamics of a terrorist operation from preparations until it actually is committed. It also illuminates the vulnerabilities of a peaceful and unprepared society, and the partially chaotic emergency response. After a nightmare-long period of approximately one hour and fifteen minutes, the shooting massacre ended when operators from the elite police counter-terrorism unit Delta arrested the perpetrator on the island.*

Keywords: arrest; atrocity; bomb attack; counter-terrorism unit Delta; Labour Party youths; massacre; police response; preparations; shooting attack; victims

Hemmingby, Cato, and Tore Bjørgo. *The Dynamics of a Terrorist Targeting Process: Anders B. Breivik and the 22 July Attacks in Norway.* Basingstoke: Palgrave Macmillan, 2016. DOI: 10.1057/9781137579973.0009.

Anders Behring Breivik originally planned to detonate his 950 kg fertilizer-bomb in the Government District at 10 a.m. on Friday 22 July (Police interview 08,03,01). At that time of the day the bomb would probably cause a high number of casualties, since the bureaucrats in general have to be in office 9 a.m. at latest. The terrorist would then easily be able to reach the Labour Party youth camp at Utøya, while the former prime minister Gro Harlem Brundtland was still present. She was the special guest speaker this particular day, and although she was not the main target for Breivik's shooting attack, he saw such a *celebrity-kill* as a big bonus in addition to the slaughter of the participating youths (Police interview 08,03,01; NTB court transcripts 19.04.2012). She was after all one of the most prominent and high-profiled leaders the Labour Party had seen after WWII, and still a powerful voice when she made one of her rare comments on pending political issues. However, the terrorist was to experience unexpected complications in the very final stages of his operation. The result was delays at the day of the attacks and this was to reduce the damage potential in the Government District substantially.

On the evening of Wednesday 20 July Breivik drove the Volkswagen Crafter, now loaded with the fertilizer-based bomb, from his farm to Oslo. Arriving shortly before midnight he parked near the train station in the street named Sigurd Iversens vei at Skøyen – not far from his mother's flat. He did not want to park the cargo van right in front of the apartment building, as his mother then could have raised questions if seeing it. Another thing worrying Breivik was that gases from the bomb material could leak out from the parked vehicle, causing smells that could make people suspicious as they passed the vehicle. Breivik had therefore prepared a company logo indicating that the car was into the business of sewer and drain cleaning, which he placed in the driver's seat – visible from the pavement side. The terrorist thought this would minimalize the chances for someone to call in complaints or become suspicious (Police interview 08,06,01). After parking, Breivik walked to his mother's apartment, slept over and took a train back to Rena about 10 a.m. the following morning. He arrived there at the train station about 1 p.m. and took a taxi straight to the farm. There he prepared the detonator-part for transport, as he wanted to take this separately from the booster charge to Oslo (Police interview 08,06,01). At 8.40 p.m. Breivik drove the Fiat Doblo to Oslo. He arrived about 11.30 p.m. and parked it right behind the Crafter for the night, before walking to his mother's apartment (NTB court transcripts 16.04.2012).[1]

DOI: 10.1057/9781137579973.0009

Back in the apartment Breivik made a decision that would lead to serious delays at the day of the attack, which was the following day. Until this point of time his original plan had been to get up at 3 a.m., in order to prepare the distribution of his You Tube-film and compendium. However, after an intensive period of preparations and the tiresome shuttling between the farm and Oslo, he felt exhausted. He therefore decided to sleep longer (NTB court transcripts 19.04.2012). Previous delays had already led to a reduced number of targets, as well as a change of the shooting attack object itself, but this decision to sleep longer the day of the attacks was to have a significant effect on the operation with regard to the damage potential. Breivik did probably not see all the potential pitfalls of sleeping longer than planned as he went to bed, but he must have seen two consequences already then. First, it would at least lead to minor delays the following day, and second, if more unforeseen trouble came along when the wheels first were in motion, it could regardless of type have the potential of destroying the whole operation.

The day of the attacks

Breivik got up some time between 7 and 8 a.m. the next morning. After breakfast he first went to the Volkswagen Crafter to install the fuse properly into the charge. Then he returned to the apartment and put himself in front of the computer. Before the attacks he wanted to upload his Knight Templar-film on You Tube and send his compendium to a high number of e-mail addresses. This called for preparations, as he wanted it to be done as quickly as possible when he returned after placing the escape car. However, he soon learned that this was to be more time-consuming than he had expected, and if not before, his time-schedule really fell apart at this stage of the operation. Subsequently, as Breivik drove the Doblo towards the Government District sometime after 11 a.m. to park his escape car, the damage potential was seriously reduced. First, he could now forget about getting to Utøya in time for killing former prime minister Gro Harlem Brundtland, who was giving her talk at the camp act the very same time. Second, it was now clear that he would initiate the attack in the Government District too late for full effect. A Friday afternoon in the middle of the holiday season meant that the H-building would be almost empty, maybe except for a few bureaucrats. However, even if the mass-casualty potential now faded with regard to

DOI: 10.1057/9781137579973.0009

the bomb, Breivik could still fulfil his ambitions of collapsing the building. In addition, the youths at the island were still there, as it would be a full schedule the day after as well.

It was just before noon when Breivik parked the Doblo at Hammersborg square, nearby the Government District. With a credit card he bought the maximum parking time of two hours and then he walked through the centre of the Government District for a last visual check. He wanted to make sure he still would be able to park right in front of the entrance and there were no changes to this. He then took a taxi from the Stortorvet square to the apartment at Skøyen. Here he immediately went to work, uploading the Knights Templar-movie on You Tube. He then sent the compendium to the 8109 e-mail addresses he had collected. However, he experienced more computer problems and later it would prove that only 958 mails actually got through.[2] Finally, Breivik consumed a so-called *ECA stack*, described to be a cocktail of ephedrine, caffeine and aspirin that Breivik believed would improve his performance during the day (Police interview 08,03,01). Now everything was set for the bomb attack and at around 2.45 p.m. Breivik left the apartment for the Volkswagen Crafter. He now brought with him a bag with the clothes he needed for the operation. In the back of the cargo van he changed to his police-like uniform, before he sat the course for the Government District just after 3 p.m. (Police interview 08,06,01).

The drive downtown went without any problems and Breivik arrived at the beginning of the Grubbegata street, leading directly up to the H-building in the middle of the Government District, about a quarter past 3 p.m. He made short halt for final preparations outside Grubbegata number 6, before moving on to the H-building. As he came up to the bomb target at 3.17 p.m. he noticed a parked vehicle on the side of the small plaza in front of the building. This car belonged to the security guards in the Norwegian Government Security and Service Organization (GSSO), and it was routinely parked there. Breivik could still quite easily drive the Crafter up to the main entrance. Bollards along the walls and in front of the entrance secured only a very limited distance between the Crafter and the building. As Breivik stopped the vehicle, he quickly lit the fuse that gave him a delay of 6 minutes and 30 seconds before detonation. He then got out of the vehicle and consciously locked the car, so that no one could get inside it and potentially disrupt the attack. The perpetrator then left the scene, walking firmly towards the escape car parked at Hammersborg Torg square, with his Glock pistol in his right hand, in case he was challenged by security guards or others. However, no security personnel or anybody else confronted the terrorist, who left undisturbed.

Just another annoying driver

It was a limited number of security guards on duty in the Government District this Friday afternoon. This was not unusual since it was in the middle of the holiday season. Most of the security guard on duty were serving in fixed positions, and only two individuals, namely the commanding officer (CO) and one security guard, were in free roles and available for upcoming tasks.[3] However, at the time Breivik parked the vehicle, the CO was in one of the garage entrances putting up some information, and the security guard had already been assigned to follow some workers in a restricted area on 9th floor in the R5 building.[4] In the operations room, the hub of the guard service located under ground level in the targeted H-building, there were two executive security officers. They were routinely organizing the shift, monitoring the CCTV system, following up alarm system and answering telephone calls coming in.

At 3.20 p.m. one of the two female receptionists in the H-building called down to the operations room, as she found the parking of the white cargo van outside the entrance suspicious (NOU 2012: 14, 17). Courier cars and others ignored the *Entry prohibited*-sign outside the building regularly, so it was not at the time regarded as a very threatening situation, but Breivik had parked unusually close to the entrance.

Receiving the call from the receptionist, the security officers in the operations room also assumed that it was a mail delivery service of some sort, and both routinely started to use the CCTV system to locate the driver, in order to get it moved straight away.[5] Since they could not pick up the driver in the live-mode search, they started to backtrack some of the camera recordings, in order to find the sequence of arrival.[6] They soon found the sequence on a camera positioned at some distance across the street. Due to the distance and the angle of the camera recordings at the time Breivik arrived they could not get a very detailed view, but they assessed that it probably was a security guard of some sort. They did not notice the helmet or the pistol he was holding, and the perpetrator's dark helmet actually made them believe it was a person with dark skin.[7] The executive security officers continued to focus on the license plate number of the vehicle, in order to track a telephone number and call

DOI: 10.1057/9781137579973.0009

the driver directly. All along the vehicle and its driver was "the usual suspect"; namely just another irritating driver.

As one of the executive security officers was in process of typing in the vehicle number for a quick-search, the bomb in the vehicle detonated.[8] The time was 3.25 p.m. and the massive blast wiped away everyone and everything on the ground floor and the outside of the building. Fragments of glass, wood and concrete flew as deadly ricochets through the air striking indiscriminately at people in the area. Documents from the offices of the top politicians and bureaucrats flew over a large part of downtown Oslo. Simultaneously, chaos evolved down in the operations room. The earthquake-like trembling and shaking was significant at the time of detonation. The monitors turned black as dust and smoke covered the cameras outside, emergency electricity power started up, water came in from above, fire alarm bells were chiming in the building and alarms poured in on the computer screen. One of the security officers grabbed the hotline to the police, telling the operator in the other end that there had been a huge bomb explosion, causing many casualties. At that point, the police had already received other calls about the explosion, but the security officer could give more accurate information – also making it clear that this was a hostile act, and not an accident of some sort. After a couple of minutes, the first ambulance and police car arrived, and for the following hour more medics, police, fire fighters, GSSO security officers and others constantly kept coming in for the extensive rescue operation.

When the bomb detonated the terrorist had reached his escape car at Hammersborg Square and started the trip towards the youth summer camp at Utøya. He tuned the radio in on the broadcaster P4 to get the result of the bombing, as he was particularly interested in whether the H-building had collapsed or not. He got disappointed when he learnt that this was not the case. He was at this time also anxious whether police controls would make leaving the city difficult. However, he had a comfortable head start, as the police capacities in Oslo first had to engage themselves in the Government District for the initial phase.

Police response and coordination of efforts in the initial phase

Oslo police district has one major central of operations only, serving as the hub regarding management and coordination of all ordinary police patrols and officers out in the streets. Receiving calls from several individuals, as well as the GSSO security officers in the Government District, the operators here quickly understood that the explosion was an act of terrorism. However, initially "the big button" was still not pushed. The consequence was that a number of potentially important steps were not taken as early as they should have been. The investigation of the 22 July commission showed that the police helicopter was not mobilized, neighbour police districts possessed capacities that were not used, the threat level in the surrounding districts was not raised, observation and control posts were not established early enough, the traffic control central (with good CCTV systems on the main road net) were not notified, the national crisis alert was not sent out and the emergency plans for terrorism incidents was not used. In total, efforts with regard to apprehending the perpetrator and prepare for secondary attacks were at large lacking, even though there were some focus relating to protecting other vulnerable objects in Oslo. Importantly though, the handling of the initial phase should be seen in the context of the time. The 22 July commission's report also stated that it was a substantially undermanned central of operations, there were generally not satisfying tools for communication and the data systems were also somewhat out of date (NOU 2012: 90–91). In addition, the establishment of the crisis management staff in the police district did not proceed without implications.

As a matter of fact, the police received a detailed, accurate and correct witness description of Brevik already at 3.35 p.m. A male individual called the police switchboard and explained that he had observed a suspicious individual at the Hammersborg torg square. Both the way Breivik was dressed, and his behaviour, triggered the interest of the witness, who noted the correct car registration number. He called in the information, also describing the direction Breivik had taken, which initially was against a one-way driven street (NOU 2012: 14, 86). The police officer in the receiving end did recognize the importance and wrote a note, before she went into the operations central, putting the note on the desk of the operation leader. The latter was busy, but they did apparently have eye contact, and the switchboard operator told the operation leader that the note was important (NOU 2012: 14, 100). At 3:56 another operator became aware of the note and called back to the witness, finally getting things more on track. About 4:15 p.m. the neighbouring police districts were alerted about the Breivik's description and his escape car (NOU 2012: 14, 102). In the police district Breivik was driving through, Asker

DOI: 10.1057/9781137579973.0009

and Bærum police district, the operations leader had three patrols at the time, and two of them were on assignments. One had been tasked to do a prisoner transport, while the other was dealing with a psychiatry case. Both units were told to abort from those assignments and wait for further orders; however, it was later revealed that they did not follow these orders. The unit on the prisoner transport task continued executing this, and the other used a considerable amount of time to free itself the psychiatry assignment. As described, the capacity of the police district was very much reduced, and Breivik drove unhindered through it (NOU 2012: 103–04).

The shooting attack at Utøya

Breivik arrived on the landside of Utøya at 4.26 p.m., almost exactly one hour after the bomb blast in Oslo (NTB court transcripts 16.04.2012). His bonus-target Gro Harlem Brundtland had left the island about 3 p.m., but this did not change anything else from the terrorist's point of view. The main target at Utøya had always been the masses with participating youths and not a single visiting celebrity. The youths were in fact now already looking forward to the next day, when Prime Minister Jens Stoltenberg would come to give a talk to the next generation of Labour Party politicians. As Breivik wanted to time his arrival with the ferry schedule he had found on the website of the youth camp, he parked and waited on a private property for about half an hour. He used the waiting time to modify his clothing, as he now removed much of the protection gear and put on a combat vest with a lot of Ammo magazines. In other words, here he traded protection for better mobility, as he did not expect any resistance or heavy confrontations to speak of at the island. He also wore a fake police badge around his neck, hoping that this would establish trust when he was trying to get over to the island.

Both in police investigative interviews and in court, Breivik gave a detailed insight in how he got over to the island (Police interview 08,03,01; NTB court transcripts 20.04.2012). He drove his Fiat Doblo down to the ferry site just before 5 p.m., where it was a Labour Party group standing, assisting the camp administration at the island itself. As Breivik parked, one person from the Labour Party group approached him and the terrorist now started acting as a policeman from the Norwegian Police Security Service. He said that he had arrived from Oslo to secure the camp, all due to the bomb attack that had been in Oslo, and purely as a preventive measure. He explained that he had to be taken across to the island by the ferry, and accordingly the ferry was called up for the transportation task. While waiting, Breivik prepared the equipment he needed in the car and after 5–10 minutes the ferry arrived. Then the female camp administrator in charge of the whole event approached Breivik. He presented her with the same cover story, and when she questioned why they had not been contacted before he showed up, Breivik blamed the chaotic situation in Oslo. The camp administrator accepted his explanation, and the terrorist then suggested that they took him over to the island and gathered all personnel engaged with the camp security, so he could brief them more properly. As the camp administrator went back to inform the ferry crew, Breivik pulled the rifle and the equipment case out of the car, and took it to the ferry. He now decided to leave the shotgun behind, as this weapon had no significant role in his planned shooting attack. By the ferry, Breivik was told by the administrator to cover up the rifle in order not to frighten the youths. He did as told and they all stepped on board. Breivik had now accomplished what he beforehand had assessed to be the most difficult part with regard to the attack at the island, namely getting over there without being compromised. During the trip over, Breivik and the camp administrator continued to talk, and Breivik now got important information about the security arrangements at the camp. He learned that an off-duty police officer named Berntsen was in charge of the security at the camp. He was unarmed, like all those assisting with security, and the participating youths had all been checked for knifes and weapons as they came to the camp the first day (Police interview 08,09,01). The terrorist nevertheless regarded the policeman as the most serious threat against the operation.

When arriving at the island, Breivik arranged for the equipment case to be taken up behind the main house, and he quite immediately met the off-duty policeman Berntsen. Breivik delivered the same story he had told the others. He was yet again convincing enough and at this stage the fake police uniform did not raise any eyebrows either, despite the fact that the upper part did not bear too much resemblance to a normal police uniform, except for the false police patches. However, the real policeman started asking Breivik more detailed questions, like where exactly he worked and whether he knew some specific police officers. Breivik, lacking knowledge about the normal police, the security service and also unfamiliar with police terminology, began to feel

DOI: 10.1057/9781137579973.0009

uncomfortable with the situation. He noticed that the policeman was getting a bit suspicious, but he bought himself some time when he suggested that they should go up to the main house for a more thorough brief on the situation there. The small group of people set in motion towards the building and Breivik was now walking right behind the camp administrator and the policeman, with a few other persons behind him. At this point Breivik thought *it is now or never* (NTB court transcripts 20.04.2012). He then raised his Glock pistol and fired a single headshot at the policeman, before he did the same with the camp administrator. Those behind panicked, and here Breivik let the ferry crew escape because they were not necessarily members of the Labour Party (NTB court transcripts 20.04.2012). Everybody else though was a target and without hesitation he shot down another security volunteer trying to escape (Police interview 08,09,01).

At 5.21 p.m. the attack had been initiated and for the next 75 minutes Anders Behring Breivik systematically and ruthlessly hunted and massacred youths all over the island, where 564 people were present at the time (NOU 2012: 14, 25). His general idea was that he should shoot as many youths as he possibly could, so that the rest were driven into the water, trying to swim the landside about 600 meters away. The cold water would then serve as a weapon of mass destruction, and he reckoned the distressed and panicking youths would all drown. His calculations proved wrong as numerous locals and tourists with small boats came to rescue the youths in the water. In addition, a number of those escaping made it to the landside themselves. In fact only one person drowned, while another individual died after falling down from a cliff. The rest died of gunshot wounds.

After initiating the shooting, the terrorist followed the main stream of panicking youths in the direction of the cafeteria building, just halting at the main building to get his rifle out. From then on he shot on everyone he spotted, both outdoors and in some of the buildings on the island. Many of the victims were killed on a very short distance, and the calculating killer also managed to trick some youths out of their hiding places, claiming to be a real police officer coming to their rescue from the shooter that was on the island. Those who were deceived by his calls and left their hideouts, or just bravely approached him to get him to stop, were shot dead without any hesitation.

The perpetrator was in general very conscious regarding his tactical behaviour at the island. As previously mentioned, he had prioritized mobility over personal armour at the island, in contradiction to the attack in the Government District, but it was also reflected the way he moved around. First of all, he walked in a controlled manner, taking his time not to oversee potential targets or rush into difficult situations. Regarding visibility, he moved so he could not be seen from the landside, due to his fear of police snipers (NTB court transcripts 20.04.2012). This is also why the trunk with ammunition and equipment he had brought with him was deliberately placed behind the main house, because then he could go there and reload his magazines without being visible from the landside. Breivik was also careful entering buildings, and especially narrow rooms, as he was afraid he could be jumped by some of the youths in hiding. In addition, he was originally planning to use an iPod to play relaxing and inspiring music during the attack, but once the attack was initiated he dropped that idea, as he would then be vulnerable for attacks from behind.

Even though Breivik was seemingly well prepared for the brutal attack, he seemed surprisingly unprepared for some of the quick decision situations he encountered on his way, and this was partially due to limited information gathering in advance of the operation – especially with regard to the age of the participants. Breivik claims he expected to confront people with an average age of 22–23 years, and not children and adolescents for whom he now literally was the judge of life and death within the split of a second (Police interview 08,03,01; NTB court transcripts 23.04.2012). At large, it seems clear that when in doubt he shot and killed, but there were a few exceptions. For example he came across a boy only 9 years old, whom he spared. He also let "a conservative looking" young man go because he seemed out of place and looked a bit like Breivik. As mentioned he also avoided shooting at the ferry crew that brought him over to the island, and he did not fire at a helicopter circling in the air during the massacre. In the latter case Breivik thought the helicopter belonged to the police, and he had no wish of killing police, since they were potential allies in a futuristic perspective. Had he known that the helicopter in fact was operating for the news media he hated so much, the decision would most likely have been different. In court, Breivik admitted it was difficult to make these shoot or not shoot-decisions, but the actions nevertheless spoke for themselves. He rarely abstained from killing – he seems to have shot when in doubt (NTB court transcripts, 23.04.2012).

DOI: 10.1057/9781137579973.0009

The police response

The first emergency call linked to the attack at Utøya came to the medical emergency line in Buskerud county at 5.24 p.m., about 2–3 minutes after the killer initiated the shooting (NOU 2012: 14, 27). Due to the content the call was immediately redirected to the Nordre Buskerud Police District's operations room. The man making the call was the skipper on the ferry that had brought Breivik to the island. He told the police officer in the receiving end that "a man is walking around shooting. He is dressed like a policeman..." (NOU 2012: 14, 113). Just a minute after both Oslo Police District and Søndre Buskerud Police District started to receive similar emergency calls from panicking youths trapped at the island – however not always that accurate with regard to information. While the local police initiated the first steps to get police patrols to the scene, things happened fast in Oslo. The Norwegian Police National Emergency Response Unit (*Beredskapstroppen* in Norwegian), usually called *Delta*, dispatched a patrol in the direction of Utøya just after 5.30 p.m., as soon as they learned of the attack. This was the very first police patrol heading for the island, but moments later the Delta-operators engaged at the bombsite in the Government District were dispatched in order to follow (NOU 2012: 14, 116). The Delta teams set the course at full speed in their vehicles, even passing responding ambulances going in the same direction, while the possibility for helicopter transport was being checked out (NOU 2012: 14, 116).

At the local police district the first patrol with two police officers set the course at 5.38 p.m., arriving at the ferry site on the landside of Utøya just 14 minutes later (NOU 2012: 14, 113). In accordance with messages from the police district's command central they stayed on the landside, observing and trying to get an overview of the situation, and also starting to make boat arrangements for the Delta force soon to arrive. The communication between the different police districts, as well as the local police and Delta units was difficult. Difference in type of communication equipment between units and bad signal conditions due to the terrain between Oslo and Utøya made it challenging to share information and establish clear arrangements for further action.

The first Delta unit arrived the area of Utvika just after 6 p.m., soon followed by other Delta patrols, but were then redirected to the bridge at Storøya, because there was a boat there for the transport to the island (NOU 2012: 14, 117). The Delta operators, eager to confront the

DOI: 10.1057/9781137579973.0009

perpetrator(s) at the island with maximum force, miscalculated the boat's loading capacity, and took aboard too many heavy equipped operators. On their way over to island the motor gave in, forcing the operators over to two privately owned boats passing by, before they could continue to Utøya. Although this unfortunate boat incident tarnished the otherwise very efficient Delta operation, in reality little time was lost, since these two boats could travel at a much higher speed.

While the police were arriving and making an effort to get over to the island in order to confront the terrorist, Breivik made two phone calls to the police where he claimed that he wanted to turn himself in. Police received the first call at 5.59 p.m. when Breivik used a mobile phone he picked up in the so-called Café-building. He dialled the police emergency number 112 and was automatically routed to the operations room of the Nordre Buskerud Police District. Breivik presented himself as "commander Anders Behring Breivik in the Norwegian anti-communist resistance movement" (NOU 2012: 14, 27). He said he was at Utøya and claimed he wanted to surrender, but at this point the conversation was cut off. The sincerity of his claim is highly questionable considering that Breivik then continued with his massacre by killing more youths. The last call Breivik made to the police was at 6.24 p.m. (about one hour after he started his massacre), and this call was automatically directed to the operations room at Søndre Buskerud Police District. Again he introduced himself with his full name, claiming to be the commander in the Norwegian resistance movement against Islamization of Europe and Norway. He added that he had been conducting an operation on behalf of the Knights Templar, and that it was now acceptable to surrender to Delta (NOU 2012: 14, 27). This call was also cut off, probably due to the technical overload of the communication lines in the area at the time. As Breivik used locked cell phones from random victims, the police did not see any number they could use to call him up again on.[9]

The final act of the brutal massacre

When the Delta operators were on their way to the island the situational understanding, based on incoming information, was four to six perpetrators.[10] They could be wearing police uniforms and presumably they were armed with automatic weapons. There were also suggestions that one of the terrorists could be positioned in the main building, with a

DOI: 10.1057/9781137579973.0009

good view over the ferry site and the open area leading up to the house. Furthermore, there was a warning about possible booby traps in the trees, and there had been reports about smoke coming from one of the buildings.[11] The CT-operators' plan was to go straight in and confront the threat as soon as possible. Both the fact that there were defenceless civilians targeted, as well as a critical timeframe, meant that the Delta operators accepted a higher risk to themselves.

The first boat with police, consisting of four Delta operators, arrived the island at 6.27 p.m. When this team arrived there was no shooting, and the team was guided north. The second team with four Delta operators and two local police officers (both of these were former Delta operators) arrived a minute later. As they arrived they could hear a lot of shooting and they observed people in panic towards the south tip. The shooting was rapid and intense.

The operators got out of the boat before dry ground was reached and came over three youngsters on the pier. The youths told to move to the other side for better cover, and while one operator stayed behind securing these, the rest of the team pressed on. At the pier area the operators felt exposed and vulnerable, and an enemy would also have the advantage of a higher position. Accordingly, the team moved fast up against a gravel road they had seen on a Google map while under transport. Moving along the water would have delayed them significantly, due to the difficult terrain there. As the operators moved up, they were continuously shouting "armed police", in order to attract the attention of any perpetrator towards themselves, and away from the helpless youths. As they advanced they used whatever natural cover they could, while maintaining a 360-degree perimeter.

Reaching the small road, the police had neither seen, nor been confronted by any perpetrators, and the group continued rapidly towards a building located south in the end of the road, called *the school building*. The shooting to the south was now less intense and more staccato, and then it became quiet. As they moved against the opening by the school building, they suddenly heard one single shot very close by. The view was still difficult due to trees and leafs, and the operators sat down and listened, before proceeding to the building. They took up positions at one of the corners, and observed towards the rand of the forest on the other side.

Suddenly they could see someone moving on the other side, but they could just see from the person's waist and down. It could be a uniform trouser, but also a training trouser, and no weapons were seen. As the individual began to cross in front, the visual conditions remained the same; just the lower part of body, and still no weapons to be seen. However, now the operators engaged him verbally, as they moved against him. The suspect's instant reaction was to run out of sight for a few seconds, in order to get rid of his rifle, before he reappeared.[12] Now he faced the police with the arms out to the sides, even with his palms outwards, in what looked like a textbook surrender. However, he did not follow the verbal orders from the police officers, and he continued to walk towards them, while chattering something the operators could not quite catch the meaning of.

The distance was now only 15–20 meters. The team leader had a good position behind a tree, his colleague two meters to the right in front had his shield for protection and the others were spread out on the flanks. They felt quite robust, and the team leader noticed that the slide of Breivik's pistol was in the rear position – the terrorist was out of ammo. However, the CT-operators suddenly noticed a wire going up his left arm and disappearing into the clothing, and the situation escalated. Together with the bulky pockets of his vest, they then feared he could actually be talking himself closer, in order to blow them all up. Due to heavy rain and a clouded sky the light made it difficult to get a clear view of the details of the kit vest. The verbal instructions continued, and the team leader had in his mind set a fixed point, if passed by Breivik, for firing. The trigger was partially squeezed in, and just a few more grams of pressure would release a shot into the head of the terrorist. Just a nanosecond before the final squeeze, both the team leader and one of the officers on the side understood that it was not a suicide rig, and they almost simultaneously called out that it was not a bomb. It was Breivik's iPod Nano and the bulky magazine pouches that made it look like a suicide bomb vest. Breivik then suddenly stopped and one officer came in from the side, taking the terrorist to the ground. He was quickly secured, while the music was still streaming out of his earplugs. Just seven minutes after the arrival of the CT-units to Utøya, but a nightmare-long period of 75 minutes after the start of the massacre, it was finally over. The terrorist was in custody.

Lying on his stomach, Breivik continued to chatter, while the three Delta operators and the two other police officers quickly reorganized. After all, they still did not know whether he was alone or a part of a group, but what they did know was that there were a lot of dead and wounded people around. While the team leader stayed on top of Breivik in order to retrieve information, the others conducted a quick search in the close surroundings. They quickly reported back to the team leader, requesting permission to initiate first aid on victims lying on the east shore, which was granted. They were also given orders to stop with the first aid if there suddenly was anymore shooting and instead confront the threat.

More Delta operators continued to arrive on the island, and a wider search and rescue phase was now initiated. In the meantime, the Delta team leader securing Breivik was trying to retrieve information from the terrorist, but this proved difficult. After a quick body search, the team leader found a bank ID-card (with picture) on Breivik, and a photo of this was immediately forwarded to the unit staff. Breivik also had 1 ½ inch spikes mounted in the heels at the back of his boots. These were quickly removed as they could cause harm if used.

The terrorist, who early on claimed there was another cell, was very self-centred and mostly talking about how difficult it had been, how everyone would understand his actions later and who he wanted to be interrogated by someone specific (probably the police security service). He was also complaining about a small cut on one of his fingers. There were no signs of empathy for the victims at all, even though there were two dead individuals lying nearby. As the team leader wanted to take Breivik's picture, in order to send an updated picture of the terrorist with his uniform-like clothing to the unit staff (also in case there were other terrorists involved), a stubborn Breivik refused. However, he was soon tricked, and a photo was secured and sent – to the terrorist's fury. From that moment, the terrorist had a face for more people than those arresting him on the island.

After an hour or so the situational picture had changed. If there were more terrorists on the island, they were now hiding or mixing with the victims. However, what the police did find was not more terrorists, but a devastating number of dead victims, a lot of wounded camp participants and numerous terrified survivors. After some time, Breivik was moved to the main building for preliminary questioning, and evacuation and medical assistance became the main focus.

In the end the terrorist had killed 69 people at the island alone, in addition to 8 people in Government District.[13] 33 of the victims at Utøya were under age 18. In the Government District 10 people were wounded severely and 190 persons suffered lighter injuries (NOU 2012: 14, 171).

At Utøya 33 persons suffered injuries due to the shooting, while many more suffered injuries during their attempts to escape, and there are still a high number of persons with psychological traumas after the incident (NOU 2012: 14, 171). In addition to this the material damages in Oslo were enormous and the financial costs are still impossible to determine. In time of writing, it is clear that a new Government District will be raised at the same location as before, and it is currently estimated that this will be finished sometime around 2025.

Notes

1   The GPS device mounted in the Fiat Doblo Breivik rented was of considerable value during the police investigation in order to track his movements.

2   Retrieved from the Oslo District Court – Judgment 2012-08-24 TOSLO-2011-188627-24E.

3   Author Cato Hemmingby worked in the Norwegian Government Security and Service Organization (GSSO) as CO and team leader for several years, also at the time for the 22 July 2011 attacks. However, he was off duty on 22 July and arrived the scene approximately 50 minutes after the bomb detonated.

4   Interview with security guard Julia Wanda in the GSSO, conducted in June 2015 by Cato Hemmingby. She was on duty in the Government District at the time of the bomb attack on 22 July 2011.

5   The CCTV system itself in the Government District was extensive and operational. The criticism of the system in the 22 July commission report seems somewhat exaggerated (NOU 2012: 419–21). Furthermore, a CCTV video sequence analysis conducted after the attacks (Faldalen 2014), fails to include several practical challenges related to operating such systems in busy urban areas.

6   Interview with executive security officer Tor-Inge Kristoffersen in the GSSO, conducted in June 2015 by Cato Hemmingby. He was on duty in the operations room in the Government District at the time of attack.

7   Ibid.

8   Ibid.

9   Cell phones which are locked can be used to call emergency numbers only, but the police in the receiving end was unable to see the number of the cell phones used on 22 July 2011.

10 The detailed information following, from the moment police arrived at the Utøya island, to the arrest of Anders Behring Breivik, is based on an interview

DOI: 10.1057/9781137579973.0009

with the Delta team leader N.N., directly involved in the arrest of the
perpetrator. This interview was conducted by Cato Hemmingby in July 2015.

11 This was correct information as Breivik tried to set fire to one building,
without succeeding. There was no fire or smoke when the police arrived on
the island.

12 The aimpoint-device on Breivik's rifle fell off, and this is an indicator that he
hastily just threw his Ruger rifle away.

13 Information retrieved from Oslo District Court – Judgment 2012-08-24
TOSLO-2011-188627-24E, and NTB court transcripts 16.04.2012.

DOI: 10.1057/9781137579973.0009

7
The Trial and Sentencing

Abstract: *For Breivik the trial was just another phase of the struggle. He prepared for it thoroughly and planned to exploit it to propagate the cause. However, his pre-trial theoretical assumptions did not foresee that court proceedings might be just as dynamic as terrorist operations. Breivik's original trial strategy was at large demolished by factors outside his control, and especially by the first psychiatric evaluation.*

Keywords: attorney; court; defendant; psychiatric evaluations; prosecution; public debate; sentencing; trial; trial strategy

Hemmingby, Cato, and Tore Bjørgo. *The Dynamics of a Terrorist Targeting Process: Anders B. Breivik and the 22 July Attacks in Norway.* Basingstoke: Palgrave Macmillan, 2016. DOI: 10.1057/9781137579973.0010.

After months of detailed planning by the Oslo Court administration, the trial against Anders Behring Breivik commenced at Oslo Court House on 16 April 2012. For the self-confident terrorist, the trial process was to become just as unpredictable and dynamic as the operation itself, and certainly far more complex than his own expectations. As a notorious planner, Breivik knew very well that a trial would provide him with a stage to be exploited for propaganda purposes. In trials related to terrorism offenses defendants normally focus on denial, or at least they try to minimize their role in order to get the mildest sentence possible.[1] However, Breivik who was perfectly aware that the question of guilt was established before the trial even started, aimed to exploit the opportunity to propagate his customized ideology to the world – and the potential was definitely there. The number of casualties, as well as the severe brutality displayed, was the very guarantee for global media coverage. For Breivik the arrest was just the beginning of a new part of the struggle, namely the propaganda phase.

As described, it was not only the attacks, the You Tube video or the distribution of his compendium that was to communicate Breivik's message to the world. The trial would give him a chance to present his ideology and mobilize support, and he was determined to use it. In police investigative interviews conducted relatively soon after the attacks, he put forward some demands, which had to be met if the police wanted him to cooperate. Some of these demands were related to the forthcoming court proceedings and main trial. For example that he should be allowed to wear his self-made military-style parade uniform in court, which was to make the headlines later on. Another demand was that the press had to be allowed to follow the trial, which was not controversial as that is normally allowed in Norway (Police interview 08,02). Nevertheless, the terrorist's transparent attempt to take control over the trial did not succeed. The fact that the trial, in principle, was run as any other trial, just in a bigger scale, obviously secured media the access the terrorist wanted, but that was it. A firm judge and the psychiatrists were to effect-ively mitigate the terrorist's behaviour during the court proceedings.

A ruthless hardliner hit hard by the first psychiatric evaluation

Breivik showed no regrets and did not make any apologies for his actions in the months after his arrest, and in court he did nothing to moderate his extremist views. The self-declared commander seemed determined

DOI: 10.1057/9781137579973.0010

to present himself as an exemplary ideal, fully dedicated and loyal to his ideology and cause. For Breivik it was crucial, from the attacks took place to the trial was over, to keep the game going, in order to boost support from individuals sharing at least some of his views. In the first remand hearing, which occurred on 25 July 2011, Breivik once again demanded to be allowed to wear his self-made uniform. However, this was refused by the judge with reference to the seriousness of the case and because it would be disturbing, provocative and offending.[2]

Breivik's principle attorney Geir Lippestad made an agreement with Breivik just days after the arrest. The two agreed that Lippestad and the defence team should take care of the legal issues, while Breivik could do whatever he wanted with everything else (Lippestad 2013: 42). Following this, Breivik's defence team initially set up a strategy aiming for a delusion plea that the terrorist was mentally ill and not responsible for his actions. The objective was to achieve compulsory mental health care as the verdict. Initially, the defendant had no objections to this.

At the same time, the court initiated a psychiatric evaluation of the perpetrator, and on 28 July the forensic psychiatrics Torgeir Husby and Synne Sørheim were given the task. Not surprisingly, the question of the mental condition of the perpetrator was of great public interest and it was widely covered in the media. The psychiatrists Husby and Sørheim delivered their report on 29 November 2011. The conclusion was that Breivik suffered from *paranoid schizophrenia,* and that he was *psychotic* during the attacks, as well as during the period of observation afterwards. This assessment was to have profound impact not only on the strategies of Breivik and his defence, but also for the General Attorney and the prosecutors Svein Holden and Inga Bejer Engh, since the report became the basis for the indictment. In fact, the General Attorney stated that they had no other alternative than to go for an insanity plea and that he should be convicted to compulsory mental health care, which also meant that Breivik could not be held accountable or punished for his acts.

For Breivik the conclusion of the report came as a shock. He knew the defence team was aiming for a compulsory mental health care verdict, but still he characterized the first report as *the ultimate humiliation.*[3] It was especially the conclusion that he was a paranoid schizophrenic that upset him, as he described in a long letter he wrote afterwards, also stating;

> *Sending a political activist to a mental hospital is more sadistic and cruel than killing him! It is a fate worse than death.*[4]

DOI: 10.1057/9781137579973.0010

Breivik's main problem with the conclusion from the first psychiatric evaluation report should be seen in the light of his plans ahead. If he was to inspire future generations of violent right-wing extremists he could not be deemed as a lunatic, and then put away in a mental hospital in some rural place. It was of crucial importance to be regarded as a rational leader, if his life project was to be continued after the sentencing.

It is important to note that it was not just the first psychiatric report that made a considerable impact on Breivik at this stage of the case. Two other important factors must be added. First, Breivik was granted access to media sources just two weeks after the psychiatric evaluation report, effective from 13 December 2011. Attorney Lippestad and the defence team had systematically collected newspapers and media reports for their client since the attacks, and the perpetrator could now for the first time see how he had been described in the press after 22 July. Going through a huge amount of articles characterizing him as a monster or a lunatic, while numerous others ridiculed him for his narcissistic personality, pompous behaviour and his ghost Knight Templar project, probably made a deep impression on the terrorist. Second, the terrorist received letters from extremist sympathisers around the world. It is highly likely that some of these forwarded the obvious point that an insanity verdict would destroy his possibilities to be taken seriously by anyone – even potential supporters.

As described, over a few weeks' time the first psychiatric report conclusion, the media access and letters from sympathisers affected Breivik profoundly. According to attorney Lippestad, the insanity issue now became a question about politics for Breivik – putting his own personal issues in the backseat (Lippestad 2013: 103). The terrorist therefore decided to change the defence strategy totally and Lippestad received his client's message on 23 December – spoiling the latter's Christmas holiday.[5] Even though the strategy for a delusion plea was abandoned at this point, the defence team decided to do so unannounced, and it took a while before it became clear to the public and others that a shift of strategy had taken place.

A bold move by the court: appointing a second psychiatric evaluation

The first forensic psychiatric report was controversial from the day the main conclusions were made public, and it took particularly heavy fire

DOI: 10.1057/9781137579973.0010

from two different groups of experts. Leading psychiatrists and psychologists claimed that the diagnosis of paranoid schizophrenia and psychosis were wrong and not documented. Experts on right-wing extremism claimed that the psychiatrists had no knowledge about the ideological context of Breivik's acts and statements, and misinterpreted them as expressions of paranoid misconceptions, although they actually seemed quite mainstream among militant right-wing extremists. In an op-ed article, professor Tore Bjørgo stated that the psychiatric report reminded him of two Norwegian psychiatrists who went to the jungles of New Guinea to assess the saneness of the locals, without any cultural knowledge.[6] In fact, both the terminology used, and the worldview Breivik expressed were of a typical right-extremist nature. Lacking knowledge about this ideological context, the forensic psychiatrists misinterpreted many of Breivik statements, such as assessing his claims that he was engaging in a civil war as *expressions of paranoid misconceptions.* Similarly, his suspicion that he was under security services' surveillance, and the measures he took to avoid detection in general, was interpreted the same way. However, Breivik was more reality-oriented than his psychiatrists as he very well could have been under surveillance by the police security service. The psychiatrists relied solely on a psychiatric frame of reference and did not consider any alternative hypotheses or interpretations.[7] These points were later repeated and elaborated in Bjørgo's testimony as an expert witness during the trial.[8]

The fierce public debate that followed the first psychiatric report, as well as the wide-open professional disagreement among leading psychiatrists in Norway about Breivik's mental health, created an uncertainty the court was uncomfortable with. The judges on the case had also registered that the staff that dealt with Breivik at Ila Prison, which included one of Norway's leading experts on forensic psychiatry, had not observed any signs of psychosis. The judges therefore took the somewhat unusual step to acquire a second opinion. In mid-January 2012 the court appointed psychiatrists Agnar Aspaas and Terje Tørrisen for a second evaluation and report.[9] Neither the defence, nor the prosecution was in favour of doing this. The General Attorney had already stated that the psychiatric report was "very thorough" and had apparently committed themselves strongly to its conclusions. Breivik's legal team appealed the decision for a second psychiatric evaluation all the way to the High Court, but without success. The High Court decision came on 15 February, and just two days later Lippestad stated that they had left the insanity plea strategy, and instead went for a criminally responsible plea.[10] Soon after a three-week long compulsory observation period of Breivik was initiated, who at this point had decided to cooperate, since he now had nothing to loose. Interestingly, the police team interviewing Breivik noted a clear shift from early March 2012 onwards in the way that he spoke about Knights Templar and the compendium.[11] He adjusted the time when he started planning the attacks, he changed parts of the terminology he used and he played down the importance of the Knights Templar during police interrogations.[12] Breivik's new strategy was in play.

In their report delivered 10 April, just days before the start of the trial, Aspaas and Tørrisen concluded that Breivik was sane at the time of the attacks, stating that he was *not* suffering from paranoid schizophrenia and that he was *not* psychotic during the attacks. They found him to have a *dissocial personality disorder* and a *narcissistic personality disorder*. In other words, Breivik was found fit for a prison sentence.[13] In contrast to the first report, this conclusion was far better received in the media and among most experts.[14] Naturally, also Breivik was satisfied with the findings, but he nevertheless felt compelled to attune his previous "pompous" posture to these new findings, as became clear during the first day of trial.

Breivik's performance in court

The authors will not address the rhetoric of Breivik specifically, as such an analysis could be a study of its own (Bjørgo 2012). However, a short reference with regard to Breivik's behaviour in court will provide a context and a sense of the atmosphere in the courtroom – and it was a head on start. The defendant started his first day in court by making his fascist style salute with a clinched fist, which many people in the audience and many of the victims found offending.[15] He also allowed himself to talk for one hour in his opening statement, which was twice the time originally allocated to him – continuing to annoy many of the victims and the lawyers representing them. The talk was, however, not as offensive and far-fetched with regard to its content, as what he had presented earlier for the police and in the remand hearings during the first months after his arrest. For example, he mentioned the Knights Templar network only once in the opening statement, clearly trying to play down its importance (NTB court transcripts, 17.04.2012). Later during the trial he continued to downplay the elite impression of the network, although continuing to claim that it existed.

Breivik openly admitted that what he said in court was influenced by the fact that there were four psychiatrists present in the courtroom. He wanted to avoid being sent to a madhouse (NTB court transcripts, 349). He also argued that the prosecution wanted to make him look ridiculous, and he got irritated when titles and uniforms of the KT-network were brought up again and again, as it now was part of his strategy to mitigate this dimension (NTB court transcripts, 349). He also admitted that he initially *did* want to use the uniform in court, but that he realized it would be unwise due to the psychiatric assessment (NTB court transcripts, 351).

In general, Breivik stayed calm during the entire trial. Even so, when an Iraqi male present in the courtroom threw a shoe against him, but hitting Breivik's assistant defence attorney instead of the defendant.[16] One of the few times he actually did seem disturbed though, was when victims and their families stood up and marched out of the courtroom, when he started giving his closing statement 22 June.[17] Another rare occasion was early in the trial, when he was moved to tears as his YouTube film was played.

It is worth noting that according to judge Wenche E. Arntzen, Breivik's ability to keep focus actually did prove beneficial to him, because seeing his performance and hearing him speak and argue gave the court valuable information as to whether he was psychotic or not.[18]

As described, the psychiatric evaluation and the fear of a delusion verdict were the main constraining factors for Breivik during the trial process; they are the most likely explanation for the change of behaviour compared to his posture during autumn 2011. It should also not be forgotten that Breivik had media access during the whole trial. He could adjust to that as well.

Breivik's trial-strategy seen in the light of his compendium

It is interesting to take a glance at what Breivik actually wrote in his compendium about trial proceedings and defence attorneys. First of all he states that a trial is an excellent opportunity and a well-suited arena the Justiciar Knight can use to propagate his case (Berwick 2011: 1107). As such, he clearly sees the court as a stage, where the defendant is playing the key role with a unique opportunity to present his ideology and views to a wider audience. In the compendium, Breivik write in a detailed manner how the defendant should behave and present demands to the court. Furthermore, the defendant should present the audience with a given scenario, and in so doing prepare both enemies and the public for what lies ahead (Berwick 2011: 1107). He gives a great deal of attention to the opening statement and the closing statement, and he practically provides his potential followers with ready-to-use scripts (Berwick 2011: 1107–1114).

Over two pages Breivik gives advice regarding finding the right defence attorney, stressing that the defendant should reject any appointed public attorney. A patriotic-oriented attorney is important (Berwick 2011: 1115), and Breivik lists three primary criteria with regard to what to expect from a defence attorney (Berwick 2011: 1115–1116);

1   Willingness to facilitate you logistically.
2   Willingness to facilitate you ideologically.
3   Willingness to facilitate you to build a case against the regime.

As described, Breivik's priority was to find a lawyer who shared his ideas and ideology, rather than focusing on professional skills. That was an absolute necessity in order to achieve a proper defence.

As it seems, Breivik was all set for a personal crusade in the courtroom, but did he really act in accordance with his own compendium? In some ways he did and in some ways he did not. First, even after declaring that he did not recognize the legitimacy of the court in itself, the defendant gave a great deal of attention to the proceedings. He was well prepared for the meetings and followed every sequence closely. He also made use of his right to comment on statements made by witnesses and expert witnesses. Finally, he used the opening and closing statement rounds as expected, but the content was not the same as in the compendium, but rather adjusted to his situation. As such, the static and descriptive nature of the manuscripts in the compendium would not have worked very well, due to the dynamics of the trial. Trials can very much be like wars; they tend to live their own lives when first set in motion. Likewise, Breivik did not foresee that he would have to concentrate on avoiding a delusion verdict, and this constrained him significantly in court.

Second, in his compendium Breivik recommended to appoint a defence attorney who sympathized with the militant ultra-nationalist agenda. Indeed, Lippestad performed his duty as a defence attorney in a highly

DOI: 10.1057/9781137579973.0010

professional manner, actually receiving considerable public credit for his way of handling the difficult task – even from the surviving victims and family members. Very much so because he did not defend the actions of the perpetrator, but focussed on his legal rights in a clinical fashion, in order to uphold the values of a society governed by law and justice. In other words, Breivik did not at all get the collaborating type of lawyer he described and recommended in his compendium. The only thing that really corresponded is that Breivik could choose his own lawyer, but the irony was that Lippestad turned out to be an active member of the Labour Party. In fact, in the aftermath it is clear that Breivik's actions and the following trial became a significant career-boost for Lippestad, who have become an even more active and influential Labour Party member in the years following the trial.

Another irony: One of Breivik's first demands when he was arrested at Utøya was that torture and the death penalty should be reinstated in Norway. A couple of months after he started serving his prison term, he complained about the prison conditions, like that he had to write with a soft rubber pen. According to him, the pen he was given was "an almost indescribable manifestation of sadism", and it represented a breach of the European Convention on Human Rights and the UN Convention against Torture.[19]

Anders Behring Breivik was in August 2012 sentenced to preventive detention for a term of twenty-one years and a minimum period of ten years. This is the maximum penalty length in Norway, but in reality the terrorist can be kept in preventive detention for as long as the court finds him to constitute a danger to society – in theory for the rest of his life.[20]

Notes

1   For more on terrorists and trials see Graaf, Beatrice de & Schmid, Alex P.
    (ed. 2016). *Terrorists on Trial: Introducing a Performative Perspective*
    (Forthcoming), with contributions from the authors of this book.
2   VG (2011). *Anders Behring Breivik vil bruke uniform i retten under fengslingsmøte.*
3   Dagsavisen (2012). *Kamp om Breiviks psyke.*
4   VG (2012). *Breivik i protestbrev fra cellen: "Verste som kunne rammet meg".*
5   Dagbladet (2012). *Jeg har ikke snakket med Breivik siden vi avsluttet saken.*
6   Bjørgo, Tore (2012). *Med monopol på vrangforestillinger.* Feature article in
    Aftenposten.
7   Ibid.

DOI: 10.1057/9781137579973.0010

8   Aftenposten (2012). *Breiviks strategi: Oppskrift på fiasko.*
9   Andersen, Jon Even (2013). *Derfor oppnevnte retten nye terrorsakkyndige.*
     Aftenposten (NTB), 16.03.2013.
10   Meldalen S.G. & Christiansen T.W. (2012). *-Det er ting vi angrer på.* Dagbladet,
     17.06.2012.
11   Hamar Arbeiderblad (2012). *Breivik endret forklaring.*
12   Aftenposten (2012). *Slik har han endret forklaring.*
13   Both psychiatric evaluation reports of Anders Behring Breivik can be found at
     www.vg.no.
14   However, the Commission for Forensic Psychiatry, which had accepted
     the first, controversial report without any comments, despite its obvious
     shortcomings, had a number of critical questions regarding the second
     report. The Commission came under heavy fire for its role in the process. It
     was claimed that it was unable to accept the second report because it had put
     too much stock in accepting the first report, which had come to the opposite
     conclusion.
15   Dagbladet (2012). *En type høyreekstrem hilsen.*
16   Aftenposten (2012). *Mann kastet sko og ropte mot Breivik.*
17   Reuters (2012). *Breivik trial closes, victims' relatives walk out.*
18   Andersen, Jon Even (2013). *Derfor oppnevnte retten nye terrorsakkyndige.*
19   VG (2012). *Breiviks egne ord om livet i fengsel: Sadisme satt i system.*
20   Oslo District Court – Judgment 2012-08-24 TOSLO-2011-188627-24E

DOI: 10.1057/9781137579973.0010

8

Breivik in a Comparative Perspective

Abstract: *Breivik was a unique solo terrorist in some ways, but also average in some other respects. To clarify the distinctions and similarities between Breivik and other solo terrorists, a comparative assessment is conducted. After a definitional elaboration, the chapter provides comparisons in a number of areas. The challenges with regard to detection and the limitations of the intelligence driven approach is also addressed.*

Keywords: creativity; definitions; detection; innovation; intelligence; lethality; lone wolf; mass casualty; resilience; societal security; solo terrorist; strategy; weapons

Hemmingby, Cato, and Tore Bjørgo. *The Dynamics of a Terrorist Targeting Process: Anders B. Breivik and the 22 July Attacks in Norway.* Basingstoke: Palgrave Macmillan, 2016. DOI: 10.1057/9781137579973.0011.

The 22 July 2011 attacks by Anders Behring Breivik were unique in a solo terrorist context, but such a claim calls for a closer look at his actions in a comparative perspective. However, before we place this particular terrorist in the landscape of other solo terrorists in Western Europe, it is necessary to address the definitional issue and the use of terms.

A definitional clarification

Terrorism conducted by one individual only has traditionally not been a main topic within terrorism research. The focus has at large been on terrorism as a collective activity (COT 2007). However, for the last few years the phenomenon of single individuals committing terrorism has been given more focus, but still there is a limited amount of in-depth studies on the topic.[1] One complicating factor facing anyone looking into this subject is the lack of consensus with regard to how this type of terrorism is defined.

Researchers are indeed familiar with definitional debates, best illustrated with the term *terrorism* itself.[2] However, it gets even more complicated with solo terrorists, because here it is also necessary to define what an individual act is. The most important thing here is to distinguish between individuals really operating alone, and cells or networks using individual attacks as a tactical choice. Then again, there are many different interpretations of what it means to operate alone. The most typical factor of diversity among scholars and others is the degree of assistance the perpetrator may receive from others. Contact or prior contact with other extremists is quite common today, physically or through social media channels, but the question is whether the phases of planning, preparation and execution of the operation have been done in a self-reliant and independent way. In other words, it boils down to whether the perpetrator has received any form of assistance from people who know, or should understand, what the individual in question is planning to do. If practical support is received from others, for example related to financing, training, weapons, other equipment, travel documents or accommodations, it is problematic to categorize it as an individual act.

On the other hand, it is profoundly challenging to assess the effect of psychological and motivational support, for example from clerics who are conscious with regard to keeping themselves on the right side of the law. Furthermore, it could be a solo terrorist act even though someone other

DOI: 10.1057/9781137579973.0011

than the perpetrator *knows* that a terrorist act is going to take place. For example, a family member or close friend might be against stated ideas or already committed crimes, but still choose not to inform the police. This was the case with Malmö-shooter Peter Mangs, who told friends about some of the shootings he was behind, but they did not inform the police (although one of them did after a long time).[3] In contrast, the wife of Breivik-inspired Brunon Kwiecien in Poland allegedly became suspicious of his behaviour and alerted the police.[4] In total, it seems reasonable to say that individuals deliberately guiding or practically assisting a person to conduct a concrete act of terrorism (even though they do not know the exact target, time and place) must be regarded as accomplices. There is then a joint understanding, or an informal or formal pact, that an act of terrorism is going to take place.

Some single actor studies include cases with a small number of perpetrators (Hewitt 2003: 79; Pantucci 2011: 9). Although there may be reasons for this, it is problematic since there are some basic differences between just one single actor and two or more persons involved, for example regarding psychological aspects and capacity. Furthermore, the detection issue is more challenging with lone actors. Also, by expanding to two or more perpetrators, the list of incidents will expand dramatically, and especially so when we look at militant Islamists (Nesser 2012). A possible consequence of this is that it may contribute to a sort of lone wolf-hype, making the problem look more extensive than it really is.[5] Accordingly, a rather narrow definition should be applied in works regarding single individuals committing terrorism offenses.

Another issue is what to call an individual committing terrorism alone. There is a number of terms describing this phenomenon, for example *freelancer* (Hewitt 2003), *lone wolf* (Spaaij 2012; COT 2007, Pantucci 2011; PET 2011), *solo terrorist, single* or *lone actor, single operator terrorist* (Heide 2011) and *lone mujahid* (Inspire 2013). Which term to use may not be as important as the definition itself, but it seems sensible to do some reflections on the subject, and maybe to avoid glorifying terms or metaphors introduced by terrorist actors themselves. For example, the term *lone wolf* has been used extensively by news media and academia in the terrorism context, since promoted by Tom Metzger and Alex Curtis in the 1990s.[6] This metaphor, much up to the reader to digest and decrypt, was maybe chosen by the right-wing extremists themselves for the association to a mythological, bold and strong animal, free of negative associations. This in contrast to the pejorative term *solo terrorist,* clearly indicating a person

DOI: 10.1057/9781137579973.0011

violating legal and moral boundaries accepted by the rest of the society. In the middle we find more neutral terms, such as lone actor or single actor. Independent of term preferred it is nevertheless important that authors clarify their choices. In this publication, the term solo terrorist is generally preferred.

Solo terrorism in Western Europe

Individuals committing terrorism without the assistance from others have probably existed just as long as collective terrorism. Before looking at the phenomenon in a West European context the influence from white supremacists in the United States must be included. In the late 1970s William Pierce (aka Andrew MacDonald) wrote *The Turner Diaries* (MacDonald 1978, 1980). It became a classic among right-wing extremists, but more importantly here Pierce's follow-up title *Hunter*, dedicated to the right-wing extremist Joseph Paul Franklin, promoted the concept of individual action (MacDonald 1989). This was followed with the *leaderless resistance* and *lone wolf* focus from Tom Metzger and Alex Curtis in the 1990s.[7] At this time, the attention towards the solo terrorist threat was minimal in Western Europe. The focus was towards the ethno-nationalists and far-left groups, such as Provisional IRA, ETA, Red Army Faction and Red Brigades.

In 1991 John Ausonius brought solo terrorism on the agenda in the northern part of Europe, as he conducted a series of shooting attacks on immigrants in Stockholm. The so-called *laserman's* campaign generated considerable fear among immigrants in the Swedish capital, not least due to the extensive news media coverage. One person was killed and several were wounded in the attacks. After Ausonius' arrest, the solo terrorist focus was reduced again, and soon a new threat was on the rise.

In the mid-1990s militant Islamists became a significant game-changer on the European continent, when *Groupe Islamique Armé* (GIA) decided to expand their terrorist campaign from Algeria to France, starting with the hijacking of Air France flight 8969 from Algiers to Paris on 24 December 1994. The following GIA campaign in France in 1995 and 1996 included a series of bomb attacks against the Metro system in Paris and other targets (Lia & Kjøk 2001). In contrast to the ethno-nationalists and far-left actors previously mentioned, the militant Islamists systematically targeted civilians in an indiscriminately manner, mainly through

DOI: 10.1057/9781137579973.0011

bomb attacks on public transport and in public areas. This represented a new, tremendous security challenge for the French authorities, and within a few years it was not limited just to France.

On 17 November 2000 Moinul Abedin was arrested in what has been characterized as the first al-Qaida–related terrorist plot in Great Britain.[8] Just over a month later the Christmas market-plot in Strasbourg was disrupted.[9] The militant Islamists, adhering to the global jihad ideology promoted by the al-Qaida Central, were by now definitely operational in Europe. However, just as it was the 9/11 attacks in 2001 that initiated the overwhelming US offensive against al-Qaida, it was the Madrid bombings in 2004 and the 7/7 London underground bombings in 2005 that really boosted the European crackdown efforts regarding al-Qaida on home ground.

From big spectaculars to small scale attacks and individual jihad

Over time the allied counterterrorism efforts weakened the leadership, structure and capabilities of al-Qaida and their affiliates considerably, leading to a change of operational strategy. To a large degree, that meant reducing the ambitions of conducting large, complex and spectacular operations. Instead al-Qaida and their affiliates had to prioritize small-scale attacks. To their advantage, however, one or a small number of perpetrators are in general harder to detect than groups. Already in the early 1990s al-Qaida strategist Abu Musab al-Suri highlighted such a strategy. In 1991 he wrote about global Islamic resistance and a year later he promoted the idea of phantom organizations, consisting of self-sufficient cells acting independently of any central command (Lia 2008). However, the call for *leaderless resistance* and *individual jihad* did not immediately materialize itself into a wave of lone mujahids in Europe or the United States. On the other hand, a transition from group-based operations to small-scale attacks conducted by one or two perpetrators came about slowly in the end of the 2000s. The Fort Hood-shooting in 2009 conducted by Nidal Malik Hasan was a grave incident, and this was followed by other incidents in 2010 and 2011 in Europe. The challenge of *homegrowns* and *grassroot* jihadis had by then been a security problem for years, but now individuals seemingly acting alone became an increasingly worrying factor.

DOI: 10.1057/9781137579973.0011

Striking from nowhere

Then, on 22 July 2011, Anders Behring Breivik made his appearance. He struck when practically everyone was following the Islamists, and the results of his actions were devastating. The attacks brought the solo terrorist issue, as well as the copycat-fear, to the headlines in the news media – and to the top of the agenda of security and intelligence services in Europe. Vice President Alexander Eisvogel in the German security service *Verfassungsschutz* warned against Breivik-imitators just a few days after the incident.[10] PET Director General Jakob Scharf in Denmark stated that solo terrorists and small groups represented a grave threat to be taken seriously.[11] MI5 Director General Jonathan Evans referred directly to the Breivik-case in a speech given before the Olympic Games in London 2012.[12] Like no one before him, Breivik had demonstrated the lethal potential of a single individual in the most brutal way, and the concerns in the aftermath reflected just that.

At the time of the 22 July attacks in Norway, the unrest in Syria had begun and it developed into a regular civil war. Initially it was civil war-like conflict not affecting too many outside the region. However, and especially from 2013 onwards, the flow of foreign fighters into the region, the expansion to Iraq and the evolution of ISIL established an increased fear for militant Islamist attacks in Western Europe further. Now however, the solo terrorist phenomenon continued to be strengthened by the fact that group plots to a large degree were detected in advance, while single individuals (with and without links to extremists circles or networks) occasionally slipped under the radar of the security services. This impression was particularly strengthened the autumn of 2014. From August to December incidents in Jerusalem, Melbourne, Quebec, Ottawa, New York, Sidney and France had solo terrorist characteristics. Police or military personnel were targeted in several of these attacks, and at large, simple weapons or vehicles were used.

However, the incidents in Paris in January 2015, consisting of the attacks on the satirical magazine Charlie Hebdo, the shooting of a male jogger in a park, the killing of a policewoman and the kosher shop siege, did not entirely fit the picture from autumn 2014. More precisely, it became a tragic reminder of the danger if two or more individuals avoid detection, and the case also displayed the deadly potential military assault rifles represent. It seems valid to suggest that the incidents (especially the Charlie Hebdo attack and the kosher shop siege) in Paris

DOI: 10.1057/9781137579973.0011

illustrated quite well that there is something between what most people call small-scale attacks and complex *spectaculars*. It was maybe small-scale in number of perpetrators, but certainly extensive or major, if the result is taken into account. Also, the weaponry may have just as much influence on the end result, as the number of perpetrators. On one side, we have often seen that attacks conducted with knives, pistols and gas canister-based bombs fail to kill a high number of people. On the other side, Nidal Malik Hasan, Anders Behring Breivik and Seifeddine Rwzgui Yacoubi[13] have demonstrated the deadly potential of shooting attacks by a single person armed with automatic or semi-automatic weapons.

The overview

In order to see Anders Behring Breivik in a comparative perspective towards other solo terrorists, Ramon Spaaij's (2012) list of conducted attacks may serve as a starting point. The chronology following here has geographically been limited to Western Europe for the period 1990–2014. A few more adjustments of Spaaij's list have been made, and the overview is also extended in time.[14] The overview is as follows:

1991–92, Sweden. Right-wing extremist and criminal John Ausonius conducted a series of shooting attacks on immigrants in the capital Stockholm. Nine attacks resulted in one casualty, much due to the fact that Ausonius often used low calibre weapons.

1993–97, Austria. Franz Fuchs was behind a campaign against immigrants and immigrant-friendly individuals, mainly using letter bombs. 27 attacks resulted in 4 fatalities and 15 injuries.

1994–2006, Italy. The so-called Italian Unabomber is believed to be behind 33 attacks using small explosive devices in public places. None of the attacks resulted in casualties. A suspect was arrested, but later released, as there was not sufficient evidence.

1999, United Kingdom. Right-wing extremist David Copeland, also known as the London nail-bomber, conducted a thirteen-day long bombing campaign, striking in public places. He was focusing on immigrants, as well as gays and lesbians. Three incidents resulted in three people killed.

2002, Netherlands. Volkert van der Graaf shot and killed politician and party leader of Lijst Pim Fortuyn (LPF) Pim Fortuyn at close range,

DOI: 10.1057/9781137579973.0011

during the national election campaign in 2002.[15] Van der Graaf was arrested shortly after the assassination.

2003, Belgium. A 45-year old Iraqi was arrested for sending ten letters laced with toxic powders, to Prime Minister Guy Verhofstadt, two ministries, three embassies, a court in Brussels, the director of airport Ostend and the port authority. Police officers and others handling letters and documents were treated for skin and eye irritation.[16]

2003–10, Sweden. Right wing-extremist Peter Mangs conducted a series of shooting attacks on immigrants in the city of Malmö in 2003, 2009 and 2010, mainly using 9 mm Glock pistol. In court he was convicted of killing two people in nine attacks.

2004, Italy. Moustafa Chaouki detonated a homemade bomb device supplemented with gas canisters outside a McDonalds restaurant in Brescia. The only killed was the perpetrator himself. His car contained four cylinders of kitchen gas, each with a capacity of 70 liters.[17]

2006, Germany. Amer Cheema came to the office building of Alex Springer with a knife, intending to attack Die Welt director Roger Köppel, due to publications of Mohammed-cartoons. Security guards inside the building took control over Cheema, who was arrested.[18]

2010, United Kingdom. Roshonara Choudry arranged a meeting with MP Stephen Timms and stabbed him with a knife when they met. Choudry was arrested and Timms survived. She was most likely a self-starter, inspired by AQ ideology on social media.[19]

2011, Germany. Militant Islamist Arid Uka killed two US soldiers with a handgun at Frankfurt Airport. He approached soldiers outside a shuttle-bus going to Ramstein airbase, and initiated the shooting. Then his weapon jammed, so Uka fled, but he was caught after a chase. Uka had online-salafi-contacts in Frankfurt (Steinberg 2013: 5).

2011, Norway. On 22 July Anders Behring Breivik first conducted a bomb attack against the Government District in Oslo. He then continued to the island of Utøya, where he initiated a shooting attack against participants at a Labour Party youth summer camp. Eight people died in Oslo, while 69 people lost their lives at Utøya.

2013, Denmark. An attacker dressed as a mailman attempted to shoot Islam-critic Lars Hedegaard on his doorstep in Copenhagen. The first shot missed and then the weapon jammed. The attacker fled the scene. A suspect (Danish-Palestinian) was arrested in Turkey in April 2014, but later inexplicably released. The suspect was known from before to the police.[20]

DOI: 10.1057/9781137579973.0011

2013, United Kingdom. Right-wing extremist Pavlo Lapshyn stabbed and killed a Muslim immigrant very shortly after arriving United Kingdom from Ukraine. He then followed up with three bomb attacks against mosques, before he was arrested.[21]

2013, France. Militant Islamist Alexandre Dhaussay attacked a soldier performing guard duty in a public area in a Paris suburb, using a small knife or box cutter. The soldier survived the attack and the perpetrator was soon afterwards arrested.[22]

2014, France. On 20 December Bertrand Nzohabonayo attacked three officers in a police station in Joue-les-Tours, while shouting "Allahu Akbar". The man wounded one officer's face at the entrance of the building and injured two others, before he was shot dead.[23]

A low-frequency phenomenon

As illustrated, terrorist attacks conducted by one person without any assistance from others is a low frequency phenomenon. Even if detected and disrupted cases had been included in this overview, it would still remain so. There is also no definitive pattern with regard to when and where they turn up. Some countries have been spared from having incidents, while others have experienced several. It may be noted though that France has experienced a number of attacks from 2013 onwards.

The overview shows that solo terrorists appear from different ideological platforms. Right-wing extremists and militant Islamists are dominating the list, while a couple of cases seem unclear. However, this should not make us overlook the fact that actors with other ideological views appear in the solo terrorist context from time to time. For example, Unabomber Theodore Kaczynski was neither a right-wing extremist, nor a militant Islamist.

Many attacks, few dead

The overview shows that a few individuals conducted many attacks, but these were not necessarily killing most people.[24] Regarding lethality a total of 16 perpetrators killed 91 persons in 105 attacks, leaving us with an average of 0.866 killed victims per attack, which is rather high.

DOI: 10.1057/9781137579973.0011

However, one should take into account that Anders Behring Breivik and the 22 July attacks was an exceptional case. If this case had not taken place, the result would have been 15 perpetrators killing 14 persons in 103 incidents, leading to the significant lower average lethality rate of 0.135 per attack. Following this, solo terrorism does *usually* not lead to a high number of casualties. The 22 July attacks' significant impact on the numbers, also illustrates the challenges of using statistics on low-frequency issues.

Even though most lone actor attacks do not result in many casualties, there are from time to time incidents with grave results.[25] Right-wing terrorist Joseph P. Franklin killed a high, but still unclear, number of people between 1977 and 1980 (FBI 2014). Nidal Malik Hasan murdered 13 people in the Fort Hood shooting in 2009. Breivik killed 77 people in 2011. Seifeddine Rwzgui Yacoubi killed 38 people in Tunisia in 2015.

Choice of strategy

Like groups and organizations, solo terrorist will normally have some kind of operational strategy – even if it is only simple one. One issue is whether to settle for a series of small-scale attacks in a long-term campaign, or to go for one attack only. This is also leading us into the question whether the perpetrator is planning for escape, capture or death. A lone actor aiming for a long-term campaign is depending on escape, and some have accordingly preferred letter bomb campaigns or remote-controlled bombs.

As previously described, Breivik chose to do a one-off spectacular shock attack, where hundreds of people were to be killed. None of the other solo terrorists in the overview went for the same strategy, and they can be divided into two main categories. More than half of the perpetrators chose to do a series of small-scale attacks, and most of them preferred to use firearms or explosives. In this category we find Ausonius, Fuchs, the Italian Unabomber, Copeland, the Iraqi male, Mangs, Lapshyn, and probably also Dhaussy. Most of them did not seek a close contact with the victims and several mainly used methods according to this, such as letter bombs, time-fixed bombs, toxic letters or long-distance shooting.

The other perpetrators chose single operations, with a significant risk of being arrested during the execution of the attack – except for Chaouki, who probably aimed for a suicide attack. This was the case with van der Graaf, Cheema, Choudry, Uka and Nzohabonayo.

Another characteristic of Breivik's strategy is the extremely brutality involved, which is not for everyone. Most people will find killing someone at close distance far more emotionally difficult than killing from a distance, for example by remote-controlled bombs or with sniper rifles at long range (Grossman 2009: 98). Breivik however, shot unarmed and helpless youths at a distance down to 10 centimetres. It seems valid to suggest here that Breivik's combination of a narcissistic personality, lack of empathy and psychological preparations, partly explains his ability to conduct such extraordinary gruesome and brutal acts. It was after all, essential for him to gain maximum news media coverage, as well as writing himself into the history as one of the worst solo terrorists ever. One way to secure this is to do something more spectacular and worse than anyone before. There is some similarity here to the grotesque beheadings conducted by ISIS, and the chemical plant attack conducted by Yassin Salhi in June 2015 in France. Salhi put the severed head up at the gate of the company targeted, in what seems to be the first completed beheading by militant Islamists in Europe.[26]

Solo terrorists and the mass casualty focus

If we look at our list of solo terrorists we get a mixed impression relating to how fixated they have been with regard to the mass casualty issue.[27] Based on their planning and actions it seems that van der Graaf, the Iraqi male, Cheema, Choudry, Uka, Dhaussay and Nzohabonayo did not have a mass casualty priority. van der Graaf, Cheema, Choudry and Dhaussay attacked single individuals. The victims of the first three were specifically selected, while Dhaussay's selection probably was related to situational circumstances. As for the Iraqi male the content of the letters was actually not lethal, which brings up the question whether the case should be characterized as terrorism at all. Arid Uka clearly wanted to kill more than two servicemen, but was it realistic to believe he could achieve a mass casualty result using a pistol at a location with armed response elements relatively nearby? Finally, Nzohabonayo could hardly expect to manage to kill a significant number of police officers at the police station.

The three cases concerning Ausonius, the Italian Unabomber and Mangs are more difficult to assess with regard to mass casualty focus. Ausonius

DOI: 10.1057/9781137579973.0011

did use low caliber weapons, which is not the ideal choice if the intention is to kill, and certainly not from distance. On the other hand, he definitely shot to kill and it remains an open question whether he could have caused a higher number of deaths over a longer period of time. If we look at the Italian Unabomber, he used quite small explosive charges. However, if the number of incidents and the lack of control on the consequences of such acts are kept in mind, it is difficult to make this a clear-cut case in either direction. The Malmö-shooter Peter Mangs used more powerful weapons than Ausonius and he also shot to kill. It is not unlikely that he could have killed ten or more people over time, but his limited tactical skills combined with a lack of self-restraint makes it questionable whether he really could achieve this when the manhunt came in motion.

Five of the perpetrators in our overview did have a clear mass casualty approach, and these were Fuchs, Copeland, Chaouki, Breivik and Lapshyn. Fuchs had a rather extensive campaign over a long period, and the explosive devices he constructed were generally lethal. Copeland was targeting public places with a lot of people. Chaouki could, if successful, killed a high number of people with his improvised bomb construction. Breivik have openly stated that he had the intention of making the government building collapse and kill as many as possible on the island. Lapshyn also demonstrated that he was able to kill, and placed explosive devices in places that could lead to a high number of fatalities.

Level of discrimination

An actor operating in a totally indiscriminate fashion may attack anyone and anywhere. The possibilities are countless. If we look to the solo terrorists in the overview, there are significant differences with regard to level of discrimination. The Italian Unabomber and Chaouki seemed totally indiscriminate with regard to victims. Setting of explosive devices in shops and public space where just anyone may be struck cannot be described otherwise.

These are followed close by other solo terrorists going after larger groups in the society, such as immigrants, gays and lesbians, religious minorities or political opponents. In this category we find Ausonius, Fuchs, Copeland, the Iraqi, Mangs, Uka, Lapshyn and Breivik. Here it is also appropriate to include those attacking police and military personnel, such as Dhaussay and Nzohabonayo.

DOI: 10.1057/9781137579973.0011

Finally, some solo terrorists are very selective and attack specific individuals. In this category we have van der Graaf, Cheema and Choudry. As described, it is considerably variation regarding discrimination of targets among solo terrorists. As for Breivik, he did have a mass casualty focus, but not totally indiscriminately. He preferred to strike against specific groups in society, which he regarded as part of the conflict, namely those he found responsible for the development of the Norwegian society.

Level of operational sophistication

Through news media one could get the impression that terrorists conducting attacks on their own are either less talented misfits of our society, or highly intellectual individuals representing an immense threat to society. If they do seemingly easy mistakes and have a troubled background, they are likely to be put in the first mentioned category. On the other hand, if they succeed with attacks and are able to evade the long arms of the law over a period of time, they soon end up in the second category. As described earlier, the reputation of a perpetrator is much linked to operational conduct, the timeline and the number of casualties.

To establish how advanced solo terrorists' operate in general is a complex matter, but one way to do this is to try to establish the degree of innovation and creativity, resulting in an impression with regard to their overall level of sophistication. *Innovation* will imply that the actor is featuring new methods or original ideas, so there is a change to something established. In the strictest sense this is so to speak never taking place. However, we can adjust it to a terrorism context and apply Adam Dolnik's definition; *"terrorist innovation is the use or preparations to use a tactic and/or technology that had not been adopted by any other terrorist organization prior to that moment"* (2007: 6).[28] Then we can definitely say that some terrorist groups have been innovative. The prime example is the Provisional Irish Republican Army, which demonstrated technical and tactical innovation, as well as ingenuity over a number of years – especially with regard to their development of bombs and mortars (Oppenheimer 2008).

Creative relates to the involvement of imagination or original ideas in order to create or achieve something, for example to come up with unexpected approaches, overcome problems, find best practice and adapt to situations. As such, creativity may lead to innovation, or alternatively simply remain to be creative, in an imitative way. As for the term *sophisticated*, this describes the terrorists' ability to be aware of, and able to interpret, complex issues. For example with regard to planning, logistics and coordination, so here we are more or less doing an overall assessment. So how can we measure this with regard to solo terrorists? One way is to make a structured, focused comparison based on a set of variables, such as personal background, targeting logic, weapons and equipment, method of attack, pre-attack conduct, execution of attack, post-attack conduct, timeline and possible patterns in their modus operandi. It is not within the reach of this publication to give a detailed assessment of each perpetrator in the overview used here, but some general impressions can be given.

First of all, the cases tell us that solo terrorists are normally not innovative, but rather imitative in their operational conduct with regard to weapons of choice, methods and approaches. Most use traditional attack methods and classic weapons, and even though those using explosives may seem more advanced, one could also argue that those using knifes or firearms are cleverly adjusting their modus operandi to their actual capacity – hence increasing the chances of a successful result. For example, Choudry had a rather simple strategy that worked. van der Graaf succeeded with his assassination of Pim Fortuyn, and both Ausonius and Mangs managed to keep going for quite a period of time due to a certain amount of tactical understanding. As such, much is up to how well they plan and conduct the attack itself. Here they often display a certain amount of creativity, both in gaining access to their target and the conduct of the attack itself. However, many also do basic mistakes on their way, for example with regard to pre-attack planning and reconnaissance, such as Peter Mangs and David Copeland. On several occasions Mangs waited outside the apartment of a potential target, unaware of the fact that the person in question was in prison. He also shot into the wrong apartment on a couple of occasions.[29] Regarding Copeland, he turned up the wrong day of the week, when he wanted to bomb a market place.[30]

In total, however, it seems that few are displaying a low degree of sophistication in general, while most are at an intermediate level, with some pluses and minuses. Very few can be characterized as highly sophisticated. As for Breivik, it is already mentioned that his strategy is rather unique for a pure solo terrorist. However, he also conducted a far more complex and demanding operation than the others. Several

DOI: 10.1057/9781137579973.0011

characteristics may be mentioned here, but first and foremost the time frame, his ability to keep focus and motivation over years, the significant operational security focus, the financial starting point and the thoroughness regarding building an appropriate cover. Furthermore, he did not take the easiest approach regarding building the bomb.

In conclusion, and returning to the before mentioned, partially media-constructed, impression that lone actors are either less talented misfits or very clever, the answer is that most lone actors, with regard to operational behaviour that is, are somewhere in between.

The challenge of detection

Most countries apply an intelligence-driven approach in order to detect and disrupt terrorists, with their respective intelligence and security services in a spearhead role – and it is the most vital part in successful counter-terrorism (English 2009: 131). Indeed, in our part of the world the effectiveness has been demonstrated by the fact that most group or network plots seem to be detected and thwarted in time. However, solo terrorists and lone actors with a somewhat loose link to other extremists, do represent a particularly difficult challenge with regard to detection, and especially so if they are security conscious about how they behave. If there is no communication with others, then the chances of detection decrease. However, quite many lone actors have some sort of link to other extremists, and the security services may utilize such openings.

For one, cultivation of informers and infiltration of agents into extremist groups and movements can prove effective against solo terrorists as well, if the individual in question have such affiliations. Then they may qualify for registration in police records, and possibly give away indicators leading to an early intervention. However, the classic dilemma for the security services with regard to surveillance is prioritization; who should be given 24/7-surveillance in a situation with limited resources (which is always the case)? Precisely who, among 40 or 50 persons, is most likely to take the final step? It takes a lot of manpower, probably more than most people think, to follow someone that close. Accordingly, difficult decisions have to be made.

Second, a solo terrorist not mingling with other extremists may use social media platforms, and for example seek some sort of social or political fellowship in chat forums. If these forums, or someone in the other end, are under monitoring, detection may be the result. However, if the suspect is deliberately downplaying his or hers extremist views, using encryption tools to hide the personal identity or act security conscious in general, the intelligence-driven may turn out insufficient – as proven with Breivik. He concealed his IP-address when active on Internet, but was also downplaying his extremist views. In fact, even his political opponents following the far-right forums, have confirmed that there were a lot of people worse than Breivik on these sites.

The tip from outside

If the intelligence-driven approach is not working, then the authorities will at large be depending on receiving the first direct indicator in the form of a tip-off, from the outside.[31] It will normally be the perpetrator's close surroundings that will notice the first warning signs, but will they report it? The answer is that some do and some do not. One exemplary case took place in the United Kingdom in 2013. Colleagues of Ian Forman in Birkenhead noticed him surfing for chemicals on the Internet while at work and warned their leader.[32] Forman was confronted with his Internet activity, but did not provide credible answers, so the employer notified the police. The warning was taken seriously and the police conducted a search of Forman's residence. There the police found a lot of compromising material indicating that he planned to bomb two mosques, which he eventually was sentenced for. As such, this was a splendid, but quite rare, example of proper reaction when concern arises. On the other hand, there are also examples of people knowing about plans or conducted attacks, where the police are not notified. For example, Peter Mangs told some of his friends about some of his deeds, but they did not forward the information to the police – with one exception after a considerable period of time.[33]

Be prepared for the black swans

It is essential to understand that no matter how great resources we put into intelligence and preventive efforts, there will always be a residual risk, and from time to time someone is bound to slip under the radar. This is a limitation of the intelligence-driven approach to be expected.

DOI: 10.1057/9781137579973.0011

As pointed out by senior intelligence expert Sir David Omand, there are limits to what government reasonably can do to protect the public (Omand 2010: 79). A main challenge in this context is really what to expect and what to prepare for, which is a difficult with a low-frequency phenomenon we get little experience on.

Most threat analysts and risk theorists will know the *black swan theory*, often used by academics and news media in relation to unpredictable events and actors. The man behind the theory, Nassim Nicholas Taleb, points to the fact that there are two types: (1) the narrated black swans that are in the discourse, and (2) those nobody talks about, since they escape models (Taleb 2010: 77). In our context we may say that the solo terrorist threat is definitely in the discourse (occasionally even hyped up), but at the same time the shape and form they appear in may escape any model. Since the past does not repeat itself, it is indeed a challenging task to try to predict the new varieties these terrorists will appear in.

Another factor here is also that solo terrorists may be more difficult to read or foresee regarding modus operandi than groups, which may have some sort of signature characteristics or typical preferences. In total, those who operate alone do enjoy a greater degree of individual freedom, as they are not affected by intragroup dynamics. The more structured cells, networks or organizations are, the more reduced each individual's freedom may turn out (Moghaddam 2006: 118–23).

Example Scandinavia: lone actors versus groups

To illustrate the problem of detection, we can look to plots and attacks conducted by solo terrorists, lone actors with extremist links and groups in Scandinavia, from 2008 to 2015:

February 2008, Denmark. Several persons, both Danish nationals and foreigners, were arrested for planning to assassinate the cartoonist Kurt Westergaard. No convictions.

October 2009, United States and Denmark. US authorities arrested T.H. Rana and D.C. Headley, on suspicion of planning a car-bomb attack on the newspaper Jyllands-Posten.

2009–10, Sweden. Peter Mangs conducted a series of shooting attacks on immigrants in Malmö in 2009 and 2010. He was also convicted for a murder committed in 2003.

2009–10, United States, Ireland, Sweden. An Islamist cell planned a shooting attack on Swedish artist Lars Vilks. Colleen LaRose was arrested in the United States. Others were arrested in Ireland.[34]

January 2010, Denmark. Mohammed Geele broke into the home of Kurt Westergaard, using a knife and axe, but was shot by arriving police. Geele had ties to AQ and al-Shabaab.

July 2010, Norway. Police arrested one Uighur and one Uzbek in Oslo, while German police arrested an Iraqi Kurd. They were suspected of planning an attack on Jyllands-Posten or Kurt Westergaard in Denmark.

September 2010, Denmark. Chechen Lors Doukaiev accidentally set of a bomb during preparation at a hotel. He was probably preparing a letter bomb to Jyllands-Posten.

December 2010, Sweden. T.A. al-Abdaly conducted a suicide attack near a busy shopping street in Stockholm, but blew himself up after a bomb went off prematurely.[35] An individual was convicted in Scotland for providing assistance.

December 2010, Denmark. Five men were arrested in Sweden and Denmark suspected of preparing a Mumbai style against the newspaper Jyllands-Posten.[36]

July 2011, Norway. Anders Behring Breivik conducted the extremely brutal 22 July attacks in the Government District in Oslo and at Utøya, killing 77 people in total.

September 2011, Denmark. Four people of Somali and Iraqi background were arrested for planning to kill Swedish Lars Vilks at an exhibition at Århus. None were convicted.

April 2012, Denmark. Three men were arrested for illegal weapons possession, and suspicion of planning a terrorist attack, as they tried to buy two AK-47 rifles.[37] The suspects had also strong links to criminal gangs.[38]

May 2012, Denmark. Two Danish-Somalis brothers believed to have connections to al-Shabab, were arrested in Copenhagen and Aarhus, suspected of planning a terrorist attack.[39]

February 2013, Denmark. A man attempted to shoot Lars Hedegaard at his doorstep. He missed with the first shot and then fled the scene. A Danish citizen of Middle Eastern origin, known to the police, was arrested in Turkey April 2014, but later released.[40]

February 2015, Denmark. O.A.H. El-Hussein conducted a shooting attack on a meeting with Lars Vilks in Copenhagen.[41] After midnight

DOI: 10.1057/9781137579973.0011

he turned up at a synagogue, where he killed a Jewish guard and wounded two police officers. El-Hussein was later killed by police.[42]

As shown, actors with different ideologies are represented, although militant Islamists were behind in most cases here. The overview tells us that all eight group plots were detected and disrupted. None of the seven lone actors or solo terrorists was detected in advance. However, four of these attacks failed during the final preparations or during the execution of attacks. Mohammed Geele, who tried to axe himself into a room in the house of cartoonist Kurt Westergaard, was shot and arrested by police. Lors Doukaiev was injured as the bomb he prepared exploded in his hotel room in Copenhagen. Abdulwahab al-Abdaly did not succeed, as he blew himself up on the streets of Stockholm. Finally, a male perpetrator missed when he tried to shoot Islam-critic Lars Hedegaard in the head on the doorstep of the latter's home. All these four perpetrators had links to extremist groups or networks. Geele was linked to al-Shabab, Doukaiev to extremists in Bremen in Germany, al-Abdaly got some assistance from Nasserdine Menni in Scotland and the Hedegaard-suspect had links to extremists in Denmark.

This leaves us with the fact that the only three who more or less managed to achieve their objectives with their attacks in Scandinavia from 2008 to 2015 were Peter Mangs, Anders Behring Breivik and Omar Abdel Hamid El-Hussein. So even though groups may represent a greater danger in form of stronger capacities, it is only individuals acting alone who have slipped under the radar and actually done damage in Scandinavia the last few years.

Notes

1   For books covering solo terrorist or lone actor terrorism see Spaaij, R. (2012). *Understanding Lone Wolf Terrorism*. London: Springer; Simon, J.D. (2013). *Lone Wolf Terrorism: Understanding the Growing Threat*. Prometheus books; Gill, P. (2015). *Lone-Actor terrorists. A Behavioural Analysis*. London: Routledge.
2   This is extensively covered in Schmid, A.P. (ed. 2011). *The Routledge Handbook of Terrorism Research*. S.39 and Appendix 2.1. London: Routledge. See also English, R. (2009). Terrorism – How to Respond. Oxford: Oxford University Press; Crenshaw, M. (2011). *Explaining Terrorism*. London: Routledge; Lia, B. (2005). *The Globalization and the Future of Terrorism*. London: Routledge.
3   Malmö tingsrätt (2011). Dom Mål nr B 10425-10, 31-32, 57, 63, 87.

DOI: 10.1057/9781137579973.0011

4   Daily Mail (2013). *Terrifying bomb arsenal of the would be Breivik who "killed his own mother when she found out about plan to blow up Polish parliament".*

5   See for example, Scott Stewart (2011). Cutting through the lone wolf hype.

6   Articles of interest by Tom Metzger can be found on www.resist.com.

7   Ibid.

8   Mackie, P. (2012). Moinul Abedin: UK's first al-Qaida inspired bomber. BBC News.

9   Johnson, I. (2002): Terrorism trial may provide details of al Qaida network.

10   Der Spiegel (2011). *Attentat in Norwegen: Verfassungsschutz warnt vor Breivik-Nachahmern.*

11   Jyllands-Posten (2011). *PET frygter flere solo-terrorister.*

12   MI5 (2012). The Olympics and beyond.

13   Seifeddine Rwzgui Yacoubi was the perpetrator behind the beach and hotel attack in Tunisia on 26 June 2015, resulting 38 dead, including 30 victims from the United Kingdom.

14   A few cases have been excluded from Spaaij's chronology since a terrorism motive seems unclear or vague. A few cases have also been added due to the fact that Spaaij's overview ends at 2012. The reader should also be aware that the cases in France are still under investigation.

15   See also COT (2007).

16   Associated Press (2003). Iraqi arrested after letters in Belgium.

17   Independent.ie (2004). Car gas blast kills man at McDonald's drive-in.

18   Der Spiegel (2006). *Karikaturen-Streit: Pakistaner verbrennen deutsche Flagge.*

19   Dodd, V. (2010). *Roshonara Choudhry: Police interview extracts.*

20   Dansk Radio (2014). *Fakta: Det ved vi om Lars Hedegaards formodede attentatmand.*

21   BBC News (2013). *Mosque bomber Pavlo Lapshyn given life for murder.*

22   BBC News (2013). French soldier stabbing: Man on terrorism-linked charges.

23   France 24 (2014). French police shooting linked to calls for jihadist attacks.

24   In this overview, each letter bomb or toxic letter is counted as one attack, as the victims are spread out with regard to location and time. This is, for example, in contrast to a shooting spree or where two bombs are going off at the same location within a short period.

25   Mass casualty is almost impossible to define in numbers, because each incident must be seen in context. Often the first responders have to make an assessment. However, for practical reasons we here say that where there is a potential for ten or more casualties there is a mass casualty intent. In our context, it does not matter whether it is due to a single attack or attacks over a period of time.

26   Doward, J. (2015). French terrorist attack: mystery of 'calm and gentle' man who beheaded his boss.

DOI: 10.1057/9781137579973.0011

27 A mass-casualty incident is a difficult to define in term of numbers of casualties, and most often it is used as a general term, just in order to describe a situation with an undefined number of casualties. In this project we have defined mass-casualty attacks as attacks with ten or more victims, or attacks with a *potential* of the same.

28 On this subject in general, see also Wilkinson, Paul (ed. 1993). *Technology and Terrorism.* London: Frank Cass; Ranstorp, M. & Normark, M. (2015). *Understanding Terrorism Innovation and Learning.* Oxon: Routledge.

29 According to investigation material from the police in Malmö, in the authors' possession.

30 BBC News (2000). Trader thought nailbomb was a joke.

31 This subject is specifically addressed in Hemmingby, Cato (2014). *Bedre rustet til å stoppe ny Breivik?* Feature article in VG 08.07.2014, http://www.vg.no/ nyheter/meninger/bedre-rustet-til-aa-stoppe-ny-breivik/a/23248996/

32 The Guardian (2014.) Neo-Nazi terrorist jailed for plotting to blow up Merseyside mosques.

33 Aftonbladet (2012). *Avslöjades av vännen.* Retrieved 05.09.2014, from http:// www.aftonbladet.se/nyheter/article14793581.ab

34 Indictment, In the United States District Court for the Eastern District of Pennsylvania, USA v. Colleen LaRose, date filed, March 10 2010'

35 The Guardian (2010). Sweden suicide bomber: Police search Bedfordshire house.

36 Astrup, S. & Herschend, S.S. (2012) *Ny anklage: Tiltalte planlagde juleterror.* Politiken.

37 The Copenhagen Post (2012). Details emerge about terror suspects.

38 It was later revealed that the arms seller was a police agent, and it is questionable whether this case involved terrorism intend at all. BT Berlingske Tidenden, 19.03.2015, *BT afslører: Anholdt fra Field's kendt af PET fra spektakulært våbenkøb.*

39 The Copenhagen Post (2012). PET foil "concrete terror action".

40 DR (2014). *Fakta: Det ved vi om Lars Hedegaards formodede attentatmand.*

41 Jyllands-posten (2015). *Fakta: Det ved vi nu om skyderierne i København.*

42 Ibid.

DOI: 10.1057/9781137579973.0011

9
Conclusion

Abstract: *What is there to learn from the case of Breivik and the 22 July attacks, and what distinguishes him from other solo terrorists? Conclusions on this, and the value of conducting research on terrorist target selection and related operational issues, are clarified here. It is argued that such knowledge is of considerable importance, and particularly for scholars, students and practitioners in the fields of law enforcement, security, intelligence and terrorism studies. Furthermore, it is described why solo terrorism will continue to represent an unpredictable threat.*

Keywords: continuous threat; counter-terrorism; learning; practitioners; prevention; protection; security strategies; societal security; solo terrorists; threat assessment

Hemmingby, Cato, and Tore Bjørgo. *The Dynamics of a Terrorist Targeting Process: Anders B. Breivik and the 22 July Attacks in Norway.* Basingstoke: Palgrave Macmillan, 2016. DOI: 10.1057/9781137579973.0012.

DOI: 10.1057/9781137579973.0012

Anders Behring Breivik was in some respects not what may be characterized as a typical solo terrorist. His hideous "shock attack strategy", the mass-casualty ambition and the appalling violence demonstrated at Utøya were beyond what most people would expect from one individual only. Furthermore, the perpetrator's megalomaniac personality is likely to have influenced his devious strategy of choice. To gain maximum media attention, as well as to ensure him a place in the "Hall of fame for infamous terrorists", it had to be spectacular and jaw dropping. The use of extraordinary cruelty and barbarism saw to this.

Breivik also demonstrated a rare ability to stay focused and motivated, and he was literally locked on target over a remarkable long period. This was combined with a solid start budget, meticulous planning and a substantial amount of persistence when problems were encountered – for example during the bomb production. Neither should we forget his security conscious behaviour, and the decision to act alone. If he had tried to involve someone else in a plot as barbaric as Utøya, then it is highly likely that the operation would have been thwarted due to a tip-off.

If we leave the aberrant characteristics and skills of Breivik, it is also apparent that he was quite average in other ways. His personal background cannot be characterized as particularly unusual, and the same applies for his radicalization process. Moreover, despite the fact that Breivik developed a customized far-right ideology, the main content was predominantly a combination of bits and pieces of conventional right-wing extremist material. Finally, most of his operational conduct and weapons of choice do not differ significantly from what we may observe in other cases.

Dynamic process, unpredictable output

Regarding the target selection process, we have explained how even a seemingly ruthless terrorist like Breivik operated under, and was affected by, an overarching framework and a number of constraints. A high number of variables linked to ideology, strategy, internal factors and external factors (including unexpected constraints and pure coincidences) were involved, and as they interacted like ingredients in a simmering pot, the process became profoundly dynamic. Breivik experienced first-hand that targeting processes and operational phases in general are not linear and fully controllable. When first set in motion, terrorist operations may

DOI: 10.1057/9781137579973.0012

partially live their own life – just like wars tend to do. Breivik became frustrated when plans had to be adjusted, and targets had to be changed. Time-fixed events increased the stress level, and with the decision to attack Utøya sheer pragmatism was introduced. The summer camp participants at the island were not eligible for death penalty according to the terrorist's own manifesto, and as such, the terrorist's determination and eagerness to act overran his self-imposed restrictions with regard to whom to kill. Moreover, and as a matter of tragic irony, the terrorist's main operation, namely the bombing in the Government District, was to be overshadowed by his secondary operation at Utøya. In short, terrorist operations are indeed dynamic and unpredictable processes, and the final output is uncertain until the attack(s) is actually conducted.

The analysis of the total target overview dataset and Breivik's concrete plans have illustrated that the targets' symbolic value was essential in the selection process in this case. In particular, iconic targets functioned as magnets for the planned bomb attacks, and unfortunately, even these did not have adequately protection at the time. Also worth mentioning, Breivik could not limit himself to attack a single individual only, as this would not be significant enough. Nor would he attack police or military personnel since they were potential allies in the future struggle.

With regard to target categories the authorities, political opponents and news media were the most attractive target groups for Breivik, and the latter as the hub and amplifier communicating the policy of the authorities and the multiculturalists. In one of his writings from prison after the trial,[1] Breivik stated that "22/7 was mainly directed at the Labour party and the Norwegian press." However, even if media institutions were ranked high on the list of targets he considered seriously, and the SKUP media conference was the shooting attack target number one in the original plan, in the end no media targets were actually attacked. Yet again, this demonstrates that the interaction between different constraints derailed Breivik from his stated goal of striking the Norwegian press, leading him to hit the Labour Party only; namely the Labour Party-led coalition government and the party's youth organization.

A lesson for Norway, a reminder for others

Until 22 July 2011, Norway had been spared for serious terrorist incidents. Hence, the focus and resources on societal security related to the

DOI: 10.1057/9781137579973.0012

terrorism threat had been limited before these attacks. This is rather typical for most countries, and history has shown us again and again that major terrorist attacks tend to boost counterterrorism efforts like nothing else. Just recollect how the 1972 Black September attack in Munich gave birth to elite counter-terrorism units in several countries in Europe, or how the Provisional IRA campaigns in England led to the Ring of Steel in the City of London. Furthermore, we saw how the 9/11 attacks boosted aviation security and intelligence resources, and how the more recent Charlie Hebdo attack and Kosher shop siege in Paris released no less than €425 million to counter-terrorism efforts over a three-year period in France.[2] It should therefore come as no surprise that the Norwegian government initiated a number of evaluations in different sectors after the 22 July attacks, which in turn led to a number of reforms and more resources regarding societal security. Rightly, some vulnerability that should be more thoroughly addressed still exists, but it is also a fact that there always will be residual risk. This taken into consideration, it seems valid to say that focus, abilities and capacities with regard to prevention, protection, emergency capabilities and resilience have been improved after the 22 July attacks.

The Breivik case was not just a rude awakening for the Norwegian government and the politicians in general. It also opened up the eyes of the Norwegian public. Until the sad Friday in July 2011 rather few Norwegians were aware of far-right extremist views and activity in our midst. The strike came from a totally unexpected direction, and few expected to see a conservative-looking, blond Norwegian male on the front page of the newspapers the day after the attacks. Even though militant Islamists, also in the eyes of the public, still represent the gravest security threat towards the society, the Norwegians in general are probably more realistic today, in the sense that they recognize that terrorism may indeed strike at home, as well as abroad.

Even though it was Norway who learnt a lesson the hard way on 22 July 2011, the attacks did have an international impact as well. The attacks put the solo terrorism phenomenon on the map internationally, and a fear for copycats and "follow ups" were soon expressed from security authorities in a number of countries. In addition, Breivik demonstrated for the whole world that solo terrorists may cause just as much, or even more, damage than groups and large networks may achieve. His bomb in Oslo did after all not stand that much back for the Provisional Irish Republican Army's "city buster" attacks in London in the 1990s.[3] If we then add the barbaric attack at Utøya, relatively few group based operations committed have exceeded the lethality, material damage and financial consequences Breivik caused.

Why study terrorist target selection processes and targeting practice?

The main objective for conducting terrorism research in general is to generate new knowledge in order to contribute to mitigate and restrain the phenomenon as effectively as possible. Furthermore, within police science we also seek specifically to gain new knowledge that is useful for the *practitioners* within law enforcement, which also may prove useful to others in the security sector as well. So what is the "added value" of conducting research on decision-making and targeting processes?

We will argue that there is indeed a practical output from projects on this subject in several areas – beyond the general contribution of moving terrorism research forward. Security and intelligence services, for example analysts working on threat assessments, profiling and reports to policy makers, will benefit substantially from more knowledge on targeting processes and practice – including the theoretical and methodological approach. It may increase the level of precision of assessments, and as such give the decision-makers or other end-users an even better foundation for their work. Let us mention some concrete examples, starting with terrorists' public discourse and rhetoric. Do terrorists on the ground follow up on the public threats and suggested approaches from central leaders and clerics in a precise manner in their actions? Or do they adjust their modus operandi according to local considerations and intragroup preferences? Moreover, do they attack as indiscriminately as many seem to think, or are they in fact more selective regarding what and whom they attack? Furthermore, which potential target objects are particularly exposed for attacks? What are the trends with regard to modus operandi, and what kind of steps should be taken to counter it?[4] In-depth studies of this kind may also produce supplementary information of value, such as how structured or superficial terrorists plan and prepare in general. Identification of indicators with regard to detection, as well as indicators helping decide when to intervene in an on-going operation, are also of significant value.

For security managers at potential target objects, such as parliaments, governmental buildings, embassies, central public transport locations or religious buildings, knowledge with regard to targeting is vital to develop comprehensive security strategies and plans. There is a baseline security to be achieved and this within a given budget. The private security industry must also be included here, as they deliver operational services, give advice, run exercises, develop physical countermeasures, work on urban area security design and so on.

Many of the circumstances and factors that influenced Breivik's decision-making and latitude, such as time, capacity and funding, are generic to all terrorists. In this study it has been interesting to note how information availability and concrete security measures (or the lack of such) have affected Breivik. We have seen how lack of information and insight made both the parliament and the national broadcaster NRK less attractive targets for the terrorist. Furthermore, the not completed closing of the Grubbegata street gave the terrorists unhindered access to the bomb target, minimizing the need for information gathering and reconnaissance. More so, due to lack of insight and a short visual observation of control into the parking entrance for the Government District, Breivik promptly dropped the idea of getting a bomb vehicle under it. In general, security precautions at potential target objects force perpetrators to collect more information and conduct thorough hostile reconnaissance, enhancing the possibility for detection. Recognizing that persistent terrorists most often will choose another target if alternative number one seems too difficult, target substitution will nevertheless mean that the operational process is prolonged. It will demand more work, activity and money – again increasing the possibility of detection. Also, the alternative targets may possibly facilitate for a less damaging and lethal outcome.

Finally, qualitative studies such as this will be of notable interest for other researchers and academics prodding in the same or related areas, and everyone else, with an interest of obtaining a better understanding of how terrorists think and act.

A phenomenon that will remain

Solo terrorism will never be a game-changer per se. It will never represent a significant threat to the existence of a state, or topple a democratic society. Solo terrorists can, however, inflict a substantial amount of casualties and material damage to a society over a limited period, they may inflict

DOI: 10.1057/9781137579973.0012

grave financial costs, they can effectively spread fear and uncertainty in a population, and their actions may also lead to political consequences if negligence or mistakes have been made. Therefore, in a holistic perspective, solo terrorism cannot be characterized as the gravest threat we face, but it is certainly a serious threat that cannot be neglected. More so, the challenge related to detection is clearly an argument as to why appropriate functional emergency procedures and resilience must be built and maintained.

Solo terrorism as a phenomenon, whether a narrow or wider definition is applied, will never fully cease to exist, but keep its place in the general threat picture. In conclusion, solo terrorists represent a constant, but unclear and unpredictable threat, and it will remain so for the future. There is however one comforting aspect; solo terrorists in general, and even more so those with a mass-casualty focus, are indeed a rare breed.

Notes

1 Letter to Bærum Police Station, with copies to a large number of recipients, dated 29.09.2013, p.16.
2 The Local (2015). France's €425 million plan to combat terrorism.
3 When a new Government district has been raised in Oslo in ten years time, the total price tag after Breivik's attacks will undoubtedly exceed the costs after the mentioned PIRA bombings in London. To learn more about these attacks and the Provisional IRA in general, see for example English, Richard (2004). *Armed Struggle: The History of the IRA*. London: Pan books.
4 The authors of this book (with others) have for example made a report regarding protection of high-symbolic parliamentary and government assets; Hemmingby, C. et.al. (2015). *Sikring av sentrale myndighetsinstitusjoner i et utvalg land*. Politihøgskolen. See also; Hemmingby, C. (2015). *Sårbare for skytevåpenangrep*. Feature article in VG 30.06.2015, http://www.vg.no/nyheter/meninger/terrorisme/saarbare-for-skytevaapenangrep/a/23480148/.

DOI: 10.1057/9781137579973.0012

Bibliography

Aftenposten (2012). *Breiviks strategi: oppskrift på fiasko.* Retrieved 02.06.2013, from http://www.aftenposten.no/ nyheter/iriks/22juli/Breiviks-strategi---Oppskrift-pa-fiasko-6840568.html

Aftenposten (2012). *Mann kastet sko og ropte mot Breivik.* Retrieved 03.03.2013, from www.aftenposten.no/ nyheter/iriks/22juli/Mann-kastet-sko-og-ropte-mot-Breivik-6826502.html#.UVc3djkdhDU

Aftenposten (2012). *Slik har han endret forklaring.* Retrieved 05.05.2013, from www.aftenposten. no/nyheter/iriks/22juli/Slik-har-han-endret-sin-forklaring-6818661.html

Aftenposten Aften (2007). *Hypotetisk og hysterisk.* Editorial, 26.02.2007.

Aftonbladet (2012). *Avslöjades av vännen.* Retrieved 05.09.2014, from http://www.aftonbladet.se/nyheter/ article14793581.ab.

Andersen, J.E. (2013). *Derfor oppnevnte retten nye terrorsakkyndige.* Aftenposten, 16.03.2013.

Associated Press (2003). *Iraqi arrested after letters in Belgium.* Retrieved 12.09.2014, from www. apnewsarchive.com/2003/Iraqi-Arrested-After-Letters-in-Belgium/id-00fb046623dcb2bf11c25e8f7e0fd35b

Astrup, Søren & Herschend, Sofie Synnøve (2012). *Ny anklage: Tiltalte planlagde Juleterror.* Politiken. Retrieved 18.04.2012, from http://politiken.dk/indland/ ECE1599931/ny-anklage-tiltalte-planlagde-juleterror/

Astrup, Søren & Herschend, Sofie Synnøve (2012). Politiken. *Aflytninger:»Dræb så mange af de mennesker, du finder«.*

Politiken. Retrieved 18.04.2012, from http://politiken.dk/indland/
    ECE1599795/aflytninger-draeb-saa-mange-af-de-mennesker-du-finder/
Bakker, Edwin & de Graaf, Beatrice (2010). *Lone Wolves – how to prevent*
    this phenomenon? ICCT Expert meeting paper, 5.
Bangstad, Sindre (2014). *Anders Breivik and the Rise of Islamophobia.*
    London: Zed Books.
BBC News (2013). French soldier stabbing: Man on terrorism-linked
    charges. Retrieved 31.03.2013, from http://www.bbc.com/news/world-
    europe-22735883
BBC News (2013). *Mosque bomber Pavlo Lapshyn given life for murder.*
BBC News (2012). *Nesserdine Menni quilty of funding Stockholm bomb*
    attack. Retrieved 16.01.2013, from www.bbc.co.uk/news/uk-scotland-
    glasgow-west-18923009
BBC News (2000). Trader thought nailbomb was a joke. Retrieved
    15.05.2014, from http://news.bbc.co.uk/2/hi/uk_news/779697.stm
Bergen Arbeiderblad (2012). *Ba om medlemslister.* Retrieved 28.03.2013, from
Bergens Tidende (2012). *Røsland: Grubbegata kunne ha vært stengt før.*
    Retrieved 16.11.2012, from http://www.bt.no/nyheter/innenriks/
    Rosland-Grubbegata-kunne-ha-vart-stengt-for-2797735.html
Berwick, Andrew, aka Anders Behring Breivik (2011). 2083 – A
    European Declaration of Independence. Retrieved 23.07.2011.
Bjordal, Nina (2012). *Breivik ringte og ba om medlemslister.*
    Nettavisen. Retrieved 06.01.2012, from http://www.nettavisen.no/
    nyheter/3305930.html
Bjørgo, Tore (1995). Extreme Nationalism and Violent Discourser in
    Scandinavia: "The Resistance", "Traitors", and "Foreign Invaders". In
    Bjørgo, T. (ed.) *Terror from the Extreme Right.* London: Frank Cass.
Bjørgo, Tore (1997). *Racist and Right-Wing Violence in Scandinavia.* Oslo:
    Tano Aschehoug.
Bjørgo, Tore (2011). *Med monopol på vrangforestillinger.* Feature article in
    Aftenposten, 07.12.2011.
Bjørgo, Tore (2012). Højreekstreme voldsideologier og terroristisk
    rationalitet: Hvordan kan man forstå Behring Breiviks udsagn og
    handlinger?, *Social Kritik,* 131, 4–25.
Bjørgo, Tore (2013). *Strategies for Preventing Terrorism.* Basingstoke:
    Palgrave Pivot.
Borchgrevink, Aage Storm (2013). *A Norwegian Tragedy: Anders Behring*
    Breivik and the Massacre at Utøya. Cambridge: Polity.
BT (2015). *BT afslører: Anholdt fra Field's kendt af PET fra spektakulært*
    våbenkøb. Retrieved 19.03.2015, from http://www.bt.dk/krimi/

DOI: 10.1057/9781137579973.0013

bt-afsloerer-anholdt-fra-fields-kendt-af-pet-fra-spektakulaert-
vaabenkoeb

Chermak, S.M., Freilich, J.D. & Simone, J.JR. (2010). Surveying
American State Police Agencies about Lone wolfs, Far-Right
criminality, and Far-Right and Islamic Jihadist criminal
collaboration, *Studies in Conflict & Terrorism*, 33:11, 1019–1041.

Concise Oxford English Dictionary, 11th edition (2006): p.707

Conway, Maura (2011). *From al-Zarqawi to al-Awlaki*. CTX: Combating
Terrorism Exchange. 2, 4, pp.12–22.

COT (2007). *Lone-Wolf Terrorism*. Instituut voor Veiligheidsen
Crisismanagment. Retrieved 10.01.2012, from www.
transnationalterrorism.eu/tekst/publications/Lone-Wolf%20
Terrorism.pdf

COT report (2008). *Concepts of Terrorism*. Deliverable 5, Workpackage 3.
Instituut voor Veiligheidsen Crisismanagment.

Crenshaw, Martha (2011). *Explaining Terrorism*. Oxon: Routledge.

Dagbladet (2012). *Breivik la plan om å arrangere fest for muslimer i
Oslo spektrum*. Retrieved 12.07.2012, from http://www.dagbladet.
no/2012/02/04/nyheter/innenriks/anders_behring_breivik/
terrror/20084798/

Dagbladet (2012). *Det er ting vi angrer på*. Retrieved 17.06.2012, from
http://www.dagbladet.no/2012/06/17/nyheter/innenriks/terror/
anders_behring_breivik/breivik/22101895/

Dagbladet (2012). *En type høyreekstrem hilsen*. Retrieved 16.03.2013, from
www.dagbladet.no/2012/02/06/nyheter/innenriks/fengslingsmote/
terror/anders_behring_breivik/20104331/.

Dagbladet (2012). *Jeg har ikke snakket med Breivik siden vi avsluttet saken*.
Retrieved 21.11.2012, from http://www.dagbladet.no/2012/11/21/
nyheter/innenriks/geir_lippestad/terrorangrepet/terror/24469707/

Dagsavisen (2012). *Kamp om Breiviks psyke*. Retrieved 28.03.2013, from
www.dagsavisen.no/samfunn/kamp-om-breiviks-psyke/

Daily Mail (2013). Terrifying bomb arsenal of the would be Breivik who
"killed his own mother when she found out about plan to blow up
Polish parliament". Retrieved 14.02.2013, from http://www.dailymail.
co.uk/news/article-2278711/Brunon-Kwiecien-Terrifying-bomb-
arsenal-Breivik-plotted-blow-Polish-parliament.html

Dansk Radio (2014). *FAKTA: Det ved vi om Lars Hedegaards formodede
attentatmand*. Retrieved 12.10.2014, from http://www.dr.dk/Nyheder/
Indland/2014/10/12/1012065216.htm

DOI: 10.1057/9781137579973.0013

Der Spiegel (2006). *Karikaturen-Streit: Pakistaner verbrennen deutsche Flagge.* Retrieved 13.05.2014, from http://www.spiegel.de/politik/ausland/karikaturen-streit-pakistaner-verbrennen-deutsche-flagge-a-414874.html

Der Spiegel (2011). *Attentat in Norwegen: Verfassungsschutz warnt vor Breivik- Nachahmern.* Retrieved 05.12.2015, from www.spiegel.de/panorama/justiz/attentat-in-norwegen-verfassungsschutz-warnt-vor-breivik-nachahmern-a-777539.html

Diesen, Sverre (2000). *Militær strategi.* Oslo: J.W. Cappelens forlag.

Dishman, Chris (2005). The leaderless nexus: When crime and terror converge, *Studies in Conflict & Terrorism*, 28:3, 237–252.

Dodd, V. (2010). Roshonara Choudhry: Police interview extracts. *The Guardian.* Retrieved 03.11.2010, from http://www.theguardian.com/uk/2010/nov/03/roshonara-choudhry-police-interview?guni=Article:in%20body%20link

Dolnik, Adam (2007). *Understanding Terrorist Innovation.* Oxon: Routledge.

Dolnik, Adam (2011). Conducting Field Research on Terrorism: A Brief Primer, *Perspectives on Terrorism*, 5:2.

Doward, J. (2015). French terrorist attack: Mystery of "calm and gentle" man who beheaded his boss. *The Guardian.* Retrieved 28.06.2015, from http://www.theguardian.com/world/2015/jun/28/islamic-terror-france-beheading

Drake, Charles J.M. (1998). *Terrorists' Target Selection.* London: Palgrave Macmillan.

English, Richard (2004). *Armed Struggle: The History of the IRA.* London: Pan books.

English, Richard (2009). *Terrorism - How to Respond.* Oxford: Oxford University Press.

Expo i dag (2012). *Peter Mangs konspiratoriska världsbild.* Retrieved 20.02.2013, from http://expo.se/2012/peter-mangs-konspiratoriska-varldsbild_5197.html

Fahsing, I.A. & Rachlew, A. (2009). Investigative interviewing in the Nordic region.

Faldalen, Jon Inge (2014). *Video som varsler og vitne.* In Hausken, Yazdani & Haagensen (ed.) Fra terror til overvåking. Oslo: Vidarforlaget.

FBI (2014). *Serial killers.* Retrieved 12.09.2014, from http://www.fbi.gov/news/stories/2014/january/serial-killers-part-4-joseph-paul-franklin

France 24 (2014). *French police shooting linked to calls for jihadist attacks.* Retrieved 21.12.2014, from http://www.france24.com/en/20141221-police-shooting-allahu-akbar-joue-tours-jihad-islamic-state/

George, Alexander L. & Bennett, Andrew (2005). *Case Studies and the Theory Development in the Social Sciences.* Cambridge: MIT Press.

DOI: 10.1057/9781137579973.0013

Gill, Paul (2015). *Lone-Actor Terrorists: A Behavioural Analysis*. London: Routledge.

Glendrange, Sølvi (2005). *-Tilhørte væpnet islamsk gruppe*. Dagbladet 03.03.05. Retrieved 07.03.2014, from http://www.dagbladet.no/nyheter/2005/03/03/425088.html

Graaf, Beatrice de & Schmid, Alex P. (ed. 2015). *Terrorists on Trial: Introducing a Performative Perspective*. Leiden: Leiden university press.

Grossman, Dave (2009). *On Killing*. New York: Back Bay Books.

Hamar Arbeiderblad (2012). *Breivik endret forklaring*. Retrieved 11.03.2013, from http://www.ha.no/Nyheter/Nyheter/tabid/72/Default.aspx?articleView=true&ModuleId=164489

Heide, Lisbeth van der (2011). *Individual terrorism*. MA thesis. University of Utrecht.

Hemmingby, Cato (2014). *Bedre rustet til å stoppe ny Breivik?* Feature article in VG 08.07.2014.

Hemmingby, Cato (2015). *Sårbare for skytevåpenangrep*. Feature article in VG 30.06.2015.

Hemmingby, C., Sand, P.H., Bjørgo, T. & Snortheimsmoen, A. (2015). *Sikring av sentrale myndighetsinstitusjoner i et utvalg land*. Norwegian Police University College.

Hewitt, Christopher (2003). *Understanding Terrorism in America*. London: Routledge.

Hoffman, Bruce (1993). Terrorist targeting: Tactics, trends and potentialities, *Terrorism and Political Violence*, 5:2, 12–29.

Hoffmann, Bruce (2006). *Inside Terrorism*. New York: Columbia University Press.

Hutchinson, Martha Crenshaw (1978). *Revolutionary Terrorism*. Stanford: Hoover Institution Press.

Hutchinson, Steven & O'Malley, Pat. (2007). *How terrorist groups decline*. ITAC Volume 2007-1.

Independent.ie (2004). Car gas blast kills man at McDonald's drive-in.

Indictment, In the United States District Court for the Eastern District of Pennsylvania. USA v. Colleen R. LaRose, date filed, 20.03.2010.

Inspire magazine, Issue 10, 2013. *Index*. Al-Malahem Media.

Johnson, Ian (2002). Terrorism trial may provide details of al Qaida network. *The Wall Street Journal*. http://online.wsj.com/news/articles/SB1018899054453675760

Johnson, Sally C. (1998). *Psychological evaluation of Theodore Kaczynski*. Retrieved 20 .02.2013, from www.paulcooijmans.com/psychology/unabombreport2.html

DOI: 10.1057/9781137579973.0013

Justisdepartementet (2012). Meld.St.21 (2012–2013): *Terrorberedskap*, Justis- og beredskapsdepartementet. www.jd.dep.no

Jyllands-Posten (2011). *PET frygter flere solo-terrorister.* Retrieved 17.01.2011, from http://jyllands-posten.dk/indland/article4600654.ece

Jyllands-posten (2015). *Fakta: Det ved vi nu om skyderierne i København.* Retrieved 27.02.2015, from http://jyllandsposten.dk/indland/politiretsvaesen/ECE7489720/FAKTA- Det-ved-vi-nu-om-skyderierne-i-København/

Kydd, W.H. & Walter, B.F. (2006). The Strategies of Terrorism, *International Security*, 31:1 (Summer 2006), 49–80.

Langset, Kristin Grue (2011). *Breivik har vært medlem og har hatt verv i ungdomspartiet.* Aftenposten. Retrieved 08.08.2012, from www. aftenposten.no/nyheter/iriks/Frp-Breivik-har-vart-medlem-og-har-hatt-verv-i-ungdomspartiet-5014741.html

Laquer, Walter (1999). *The New Terrorism.* Oxford: Oxford University Press.

Lia, Brynjar (2005). *The Globalization and the Future of Terrorism.* London: Routledge.

Lia, Brynjar (2008). *Architect of Global Jihad.* New York: Columbia University Press.

Lia, Brynjar & Kjøk, Åshild (2001). *Islamist Insurgencies, diasporic support networks, and their host states: The Case of the Algerian GIA in Europe 1993–2000.* FFI Report 2001/03789. Forsvarets forskningsinstitutt.

Lippestad, Geir (2013). *Det kan vi stå for.* Oslo: Aschehoug.

Macdonald, Andrew (2nd ed. 1980). *The Turner Diaries.* Hillsboro: National Vanguard Books.

Macdonald, Andrew (1989). *Hunter.* Hillsboro: National Vanguard Books.

Mackie, P. (2012). Moinul Abedin: UK's first al-Qaeda inspired bomber. BBC News. Retrieved 05.02.2013, from http://www.bbc.co.uk/news/uk-england-birmingham- 17231013

Mahnken, Thomas G. (2010). Strategic theory. In Baylis et.al (3rd ed.) *Strategy in the Contemporary world.* Oxford: Oxford University Press.

Malmö tingsrätt (2011). Dom Mål nr B 10425-10. Malmö.

Matusitz, Jonathan (2015). *Symbolism in Terrorism: Motivation, Communication and Behavior.* London: Rowman & Littlefield.

Meldalen S.G. & Christiansen T.W. (2012). -*Det er ting vi angrer på.* Dagbladet, 17.06.2012.

MI5. (2012). *The Olympics and beyond.* Retrieved 17.12.2012, from www. mi5.gov.uk/home/about-us/who-we-are/staff-and-management/director-general/speeches-by-the-director-general/the-olympics-and-beyond.html

DOI: 10.1057/9781137579973.0013

Michael, George (2012). *Lone Wolf Terrorism and the Rise of Leaderless Resistance*. Nashville: Vanderbilt.

Moghaddam, Fathali M. (2006). *From the Terrorists' Point of View*. Westport: Praeger.

Moghaddam, Fathali M. (2008). *How Globalization Spurs Terrorism*. Westport: Praeger.

Nesser, Petter (2012). *Individual jihadist operations in Europe: Patterns and challenges*. Retrieved 20.01.2012, from www.ctc.usma.edu

Nettavisen (2010). *Al-Qaida medlemmer pågrepet i Norge*. Retrieved 01.02.2013, from www.nettavisen.no/nyheter/article2941616.ece

Nordal, S. & Halkjelsvik, S. (2011). *Vurderte å leige jord til Behring Breivik*. Retrieved 20.07.2015, from http://www.smp.no/nyheter/soere/article371469.ece

NOU 2012:14. *Rapport fra 22.juli-kommisjonen*. Oslo.

NRK (2012). *Lippestad: Vurderer å be om utsettelse av saken*. Retrieved 16.04.2012, from http://www.nrk.no/227/dag-for-dag/forsvarerne-vil-kanskje-utsette-1.8076216

NRK Østlandssendingen (2006). *Advarte om bomben i 2006*. Retrieved 10.04.2014, from http://www.nrk.no/ostlandssendingen/advarte-om-bomben-i-2006-1.7737572

NTB Norwegian News Agency (2012). Word for word – transcripts from the 22 July trial.

Omand, David (2010). *Securing the State*. London: C. Hurst.

Oppenheimer, Andy R. (2008). *The Bombs and the Bullets*. Sallins: Irish Academic Press.

Oslo District Court (2012). Judgment 2012-08-24 TOSLO-2011-188627-24E.

Oslo Police District (2011–2012). Transcripts of the police interviews of Anders B. Breivik.

Pantucci, Raffaello (2011). *A Typology of Lone Wolves*. ICSR Kings College.

Politiets efterretningstjeneste (2011). *The threat from solo terrorism and lone wolf terrorism*. www.pet.dk

Ranstorp, Magnus & Normark, Magnus (2015). *Understanding Terrorism Innovation and Learning*. Oxon: Routledge.

Rapoport, David C. (ed. 2001). *Inside Terrorist Organizations*. London: Frank Cass.

Reuters (2012). Breivik trial closes, victims' relatives walk out. Retrieved 22.06.2012, from www.reuters.com/article/2012/06/22/us-breivik-trial-idUSBRE85L0CM20120622.

DOI: 10.1057/9781137579973.0013

Ringheim, G. (2009). *NRK-Takvam er mye hardere mot Siv enn Kristin.* Retrieved 12.05.2012, from www.dagbladet.no/2009/09/04/nyheter/valg_2009/valg09/politikk/innenriks/7953821/

Sandnes, Cathrine (2012). *«Blir vi et bedre samfunn av å sparke folk til de ikke reiser seg igjen?».* Feature article in Dagbladet. Retrieved 14.07.2015, from http://www.dagbladet.no/2012/09/01/kultur/debatt/kommentar/erlig_talt/lordagskommentaren/23204716/

Schelling (2008). *Arms and influence.* In Mahnken and Maiolo (eds.), *Strategic Studies.* Oxon: Routledge.

Schmid, Alex P. (ed. 2011). *The Routledge Handbook of Terrorism Research.* London: Routledge.

Schuurman, Bart & Eijkman, Quirine (2015). Indicators of terrorist intent and capability: Tools for threat assessment. Dynamics of Asymmetric Conflict: Pathways toward terrorism and genocide, http//dx.doi.org/10.1080/17467586.2015.1040426

Seierstad, Åsne (2015). *One of Us.* London: Virago.

Simon, J.D. (2013). *Lone Wolf Terrorism: Understanding the Growing Threat.* Prometheus books.

Spaaij, Ramon (2012). *Understanding Lone Wolf Terrorism.* London: Springer.

Stewart, Scott (2011). Cutting through the lone wolf hype. Retrieved 10.03.2014, from https://www.stratfor.com/weekly/20110921-cutting-through-lone-wolf-hype

The Copenhagen Post (2012). Details emerge about terror suspects. Retrieved 30.04.2012, from http://cphpost.dk/news/details-emerge-about-terror-suspects.1455.html

The Copenhagen Post (2012). PET foil "concrete terror action". Retrieved 15.01.2014, from http://cphpost.dk/news/pet-foil-concrete-terror-action.1747.html

The Guardian (2010). Sweden suicide bomber: Police search Bedfordshire house. Retrieved 13.12.2010, from http://www.theguardian.com/world/2010/dec/13/sweden-suicide-bomber-bedfordshire-house

The Guardian (2014). Nantes Christmas shoppers hurt as man drives van into crowd. Retrieved 22.12.2014, from http://www.theguardian.com/world/2014/dec/22/nantes-christmas-shoppers-hurtman--drives-van-into-crowd

The Guardian (2014). Neo-Nazi terrorist jailed for plotting to blow up Merseyside Mosques. Retrieved 01.05.2014, from http://www.theguardian.com/uk-news/2014/may/01/neo-nazi-terrorist-merseyside-mosques-ian-forman

DOI: 10.1057/9781137579973.0013

The Local (2015). France's €425 million plan to combat terrorism. Retrieved 21.01.2015, from http://www.thelocal.fr/20150121/france-terrorism-valls-jihadists-surveillance

The Mirror (2014). Dijon "terror" attack: 11 injured as psychiatric patient drives into crowd "shouting Islamic slogans". Retrieved 21.12.2014, from http://www.mirror.co.uk/news/world-news/dijon-terror-attack-11-injured-4851540

Thornton, T.P. (1965). Terror as a Weapon of Political Agitation. In H. Eckstein (ed.) *Internal War*. New York: The Free Press of Glencoe.

Tom Williamson, Becky Milne & Stephen Savage (ed.) *International developments in investigative interviewing*, 39–65. Collumpton: Willan.

United States District Court for the Eastern District of Pennsylvania, Indictment, USA v. Colleen R. LaRose, date filed, 10.03.2010, http://media.nbcphiladelphia.com/documents/JihadJane.pdf

VG (2012). *Breivik i protestbrev fra cellen: "Verste som kunne rammet meg"*. Retrieved 03.02.2013, from http://www.vg.no/nyheter/innenriks/22-juli/artikkel.php?artid=10049584

VG Nett (2011). *Anders Behring Breivik vil bruke uniform i rette under fengslingsmøte*. Retrieved 15.03.2012, from www.vg.no/nyheter/utskrift svennlig/?artId=10080740

VG Nett (2012). *Breivik er en over gjennomsnittet kompetent terrorist*. Retrieved 15.02.2013, from http://www.vg.no/nyheter/innenriks/terrorangrepet-22-juli-rettssaken/professor-breivik-er-en-over-gjennomsnittet-kompetent-terrorist/a/10053976/

VG Nett (2012). *Breiviks egne ord fra fengselscellen*. Retrieved 22.06.2012, from http://www.vg.no/nyheter/innenriks/22-juli/artikkel.php?artid=10064799

VG Nett (2012). *Breiviks egne ord om livet i fengsel: Sadisme satt i system*. Retrieved 05.03.2013, from http://www.vg.no/nyheter/innenriks/22-juli/artikkel.php?artid=10055585

VG Nett (2012). *Foreløpig psykiatrisk vurdering av forhold rundt Anders Behring Breivik*. A report by Randi Rosenqvist. Published by newspaper VG, retrieved 06.06.2012, from http://www.vg.no/nyheter/innenriks/22-juli/psykiatrisk_vurdering/

VG Nett (2012). *Ord-for-ord, dag 43*, 17.04.2012. Retrieved 27.09.2014, from http://www.vg.no/nyheter/innenriks/terrorangrepet-22-juli-rettssaken/ord-for-ord-dag-43/a/10051118/

Wilkinson, Paul (ed. 1993). *Technology and Terrorism*. London: Frank Cass.

DOI: 10.1057/9781137579973.0013

Index

DOI: 10.1057/9781137579973.0014

DOI: 10.1057/9781137579973.0014

DOI: 10.1057/9781137579973.0014

DOI: 10.1057/9781137579973.0014

DOI: 10.1057/9781137579973.0014

CPSIA information can be obtained
at www.ICGtesting.com
Printed in the USA
LVOW11*0851110318
569449LV00007B/735/P

.